WITHDRAWN
HARVARD LIBRARY
WITHDRAWN

LISTEN
METAPHYSICS

THE SEMANTICS OF REALITY

LISTEN
METAPHYSICS
THE SEMANTICS OF REALITY

by

FRANK S. MERRITT

PHILOSOPHICAL LIBRARY
New York

Copyright, © 1974, by Philosophical Library, Inc.,
15 East 40th Street, New York, N. Y. 10016

All rights reserved

Library of Congress Catalog Card No. 73-77407
SBN 8022-2118-1

Printed in United States of America

BD
111
.M53

CONTENTS

Chapter		Page
I	WHY METAPHYSICS?	1
	Off Balance of the New Age of Light and Reason	4
II	WHAT ARE OUR STANDARDS?	29
	The Christian Era	31
	The Advance of Science and Technology	36
III	THE TRIANGLE OF THE CREATIVE PROCESS	41
	Spiritual-Mental-Physical Warning approach of the New Era	48
IV	LOOKING WITH IMPUNITY OF UNDERSTANDING	53
	Merging Cusp of Change	57
	Limitations of Traditional Religion	58
	Negative Thought, The Destroyer	66
V	UNIVERSAL LAW Vs. SUPERSTITION	69
	Ancient Symbols of the Ages	76
	(See plate on page 183)	
	The Spirit of the Letter	86
VI	METAPHYSICS — THE AMALGAMATING PRINCIPLE	101
	The Authenticity of the Zodiac	102
	"He That is not Against Me is For Me"	108

VII	THE IMPLICATION OF METAPHYSICS IN POVERTY AND DISTRESS	109
	Metaphysics, the Soul's Survival	111
VIII	BY WHAT AUTHORITY?	121
	Detailed Description of the Creative Process	137
	A few Axioms of Principle	139
IX	BUILDING A NEW OUTLOOK	141
	Part II Summary	150
X	GLOSSARY OF TERMS AND THEIR MEANING AS USED IN THIS TREATISE	175
	Freedom of Choice — God's Gift to Man	185
	"CYCLE OF BEING" (A Poem)	186
	FINIS	187

FOREWORD

One of the wisest and most meaningful utterances coming down to us through the centuries is that purported to have been made by King Solomon. "With all thy getting, get understanding" — the writer believes Solomon. Considered understanding of Universal Laws was of first importance, for they must constitute the only safe guiding principles governing in every segment of creation.

The Master Teacher, Jesus, taught that the souls of mankind were inseparably linked with the Spirit of God and that the Creative Christ Principle that indwells us all is the medium through which manifestation results from thoughts we think with conviction, as far as our personal world is concerned.

It is evident that millions of souls that populate this globe have missed the significance of Solomon's Divinely prompted advice, concerning the "Spirit of Reality" and its laws.

The contents of this book dwell upon the abstract "First Causes" and their inevitable effects — especially when they run counter to Standard Universal Principles and how the creative power of thought wrongly used is again digging the pit that has tumbled past generations to their end.

The writer rationalizes, under established principles, what must be done to turn the tide of error which inevitably spells destruction under the Law of "Cause and Effect." The "so called" cyclic Age of Aquarius — "the Age of New Thought," is upon us now!

He has titled his book "LISTEN" because he feels it

stands for the "key" most important to the seeker of clearer concepts of Reality.

In this regard, for those desiring more *authenticated* facts concerning the subject offered here, he wholeheartedly recommends Mrs. Lucille DeMerchman's authenticated researched book "New Light Upon Old Tradition." This is a recent publication by "Devores." (This is not a solicited announcement by the author or the publisher of Mrs. DeMerchman's book.)

L - I - S - T - E - N

"Listen" — That's a lovely word —
It makes one quiet and still —
There is so much good in the world to hear,
The birds that chirp and trill —
The wild winds fluting in the trees —
The drumming of the rain — The muffled
Fluttering of the moths on the window pane:
Then too:

There's Chopin, Beethoven, Liszt, and Grieg —
Giants of music's art — that created
Golden melodies to stir the human heart.

Oh yes,
The world is full of lovely sounds —
But not so full I ween, there's no room left
For dark — that rarely ever gleams.

It seems,
Nature provides a pinch of salt —
For every bowl of love — a bit of hell
For every heaven above — is not this so?

'Tis said:
Life would lose its savor and contrasts
Could not be, if everything was lovely,
Now, can not you agree?

Does not
Love's most coveted treasure oft
Bide among things we would not hear —
Things that serve and not to fear?

So close your eyes and listen —
After you've read a few lines herein —
You will hear all kinds of things —
From the deep down wells within —
Somethings will perchance, disturb
The waters of calm repose — but did not
God create the asp as also did He the rose?
Frank S. Merritt

CHAPTER I

WHY METAPHYSICS

The reason is Simple: Because Metaphysics deals with the only creative power in existence — namely: *"Thought Power"* which is *"Idea Power."*
Thought manifests an idea and the idea determines the purpose of every conceivable manifestation in existence.
Man has been given freedom of choice — *not the power* that enables him to put into effect any idea he chooses — right or wrong. It is the Life Principle that indwells him and every soul of mankind.
Without which, again, the consciousness which we call our own does not exist. I repeat, "Man is the instrumentality that Divine Mind designed to carry out Its Plan." Mankind must come to understand his purpose in life *"progressively,"* for Progress is the Universal Law governing all Creation. In reality, man's mind is one with God's Mind. All that he creates — he does so, in the "Name of the Father."
It is the *spirit* of the *letter* of our Scriptures that has to be understood — mentally. (Metaphysically). It isn't a lullaby to put one to sleep concerning things taking place around us and the world.
Many people searching for escape from serious types of unhappiness of their own engendered mental-making — they find it hard to realize that thoughts are forever creating something through the spiritual mechanism God has endowed us with, namely, the conscious and sub-conscious

minds which are nonetheless God's Mind, and as I have inferred in other parts of this message: There is no separation in the reality of Mind.

Our surface thoughts have a tendency to congeal into convictions and it's our convictions that determine the nature of the things we are attracting to ourselves, as the world about us.

The Scriptures assure us: "As a man thinketh in his heart, (or deeply) so he is." It follows, through the law of "Attraction," or reflection, our world faithfully mirrors back our real thinking-self.

Conscious understanding does not rob one of the pleasures the world has to offer. It does protect us from many pitfalls through our ignorance of *First Causes*.

Placing dependence upon *material standards* for real guidance, which, even our Physical Sciences find necessary to modify, every time Technology discovers another *fact-of-life's effects* which, on the face of it, *are not reliable in the reach of time and space.*

Physical Science has not been able to predict the limits of outer space. Nor has "Materia Medica" been able, one infinitesimal degree, to explain, much less alter, the nature of the Power that enables one to visualize the material about us. What these sciences can do, is break down the atom into its component parts and give these parts names. But it takes the imagination and *discernment* or *Metaphysics* to really understand what goes on behind the scene. In other words, the *Life Principle* indwells every atom that comes into existence. It is the Intelligence that moves the instincts of all nature. It knows why and for what purpose every atom of creation exists. One cannot successfully transplant one cell or organ into any part not designed for it.

We may ask where the outside of Creation is located. There is but one correct answer: In Divine Mind. There is no physical outline that one can physically visualize.

Only through mental discernment or, again, through metaphysics can one conclude the truth.

This great Truth is open to all normal *human* beings, but it must be paid for, through open minded effort.

You have read: The sins (or ignorance) of our forefathers are visited upon the children unto the 3rd and 4th generation. This bespeaks that it takes more than one "class room" so to speak, for a soul to learn the laws of life.

One can rest assured, God did not make a mistake in His plans for multiplying and extending His creativity.

One cannot assume a creature can be developed into an image of His creator outside the Law of Progression.

I will no doubt repeat, in this essay, that there is no such thing as an accident in all Creation. If there appears to be a cause, it is only a secondary cause. What "understanding" has come to know *through the Universal Standard life laws* is that all effects, whether constructive or not, rest with the original idea. If an idea is constructive, the effects will be constructive and vice versa.

It is the spiritual essence of the Master's teaching that has been misunderstood. As I have said before, mankind has been enslaved through the misinterpretation of the *letter* of its Bibles.

Witness a prime example in the deeply religious country of Ireland. The people have accepted the teachings of, mainly, two religious institutions. Both professing Christian doctrine — *according* to the *letter* of their Bibles — not the Spirit, for God does not compete with Himself.

Competition is an animal law, perfectly understood, in building animal bodies, including our own.

The same lack of understanding is back of civilization's troubles today! So again, it is the incorrect teaching of civilization's moral textbooks. *That* is what this book is all about.

Truth is Reality and Reality is the Eternal, never changing spirit of life which, in turn, is God.

As I have said above, understanding comes progressively. It is the mental pathway mankind must take.

Traditional stagnation does not meet the Divine Law of "progression."

Once one becomes fully abreast of the implications of metaphysics, he will have, indeed a freedom and knowledge of where he is going and the truth of what is happening in the world today — because of a lack of that *understanding* which was proclaimed two thousand years ago as the most precious possession one could have.

The nearer one cleaves to Universal Standard Laws, the nearer one approaches the perfect balance which is the nature of Divine Mind.

OFF BALANCE OF THE NEW AGE OF LIGHT & REASON

Equilibrium must be the nature of The Divine Mind of God. Expressed in terms of the English language means: *"Perfect Balance"* or "I" or stillness — no movement.

Back track *heat* to its Source and we find perfect *"coldness"*. Back track any or all of the colors of the spectrum and we find *pure white*. Back track the end terminal of any of the billion rays of the Solar Orb to its source, which is the indwelling center of the Sun, and we find the pure white light of Supreme Intelligence — The Mind of God.

The number of vibratory impulses of a single ray of the Sun determines the nature of the object it supports in the objective world of nature.

The crucial question is: How off balance from the nature of Divine Mind is our human civilization today?

The news media and every channel of information the public *enjoys* or *laments*, keeps us informed of the need for a constructive look to other Sources than that which we find is leading to disaster.

The proof? The Universal Principle of *Cause and Effect*. The effects we are witnessing — The *first Cause* is what I discern and am trying to explain within these pages.

If our Base Principles are correct, they hold the answer to the riddle of our times, and again they can be summed up in just one word: *"Understanding"*.

If you believe in Christianity and hold to its book of morals, then you must believe that King Solomon knew what he was talking about when he said: *"With all thy getting get Understanding"*.

This bit of advice tells us that we do not have understanding without learning and learning is progressive.

Jesus was supporting this truism when He said: "The poor will be with us always". The poor in understanding are coming into the world continually.

Every department of life is under the Divine Standard of Progression. Even the souls of mankind have to learn the Father's Laws progressively, before one could match God's laws which do not conflict with any other of His ordinances.

Such as the sacrifice of the Father's only Son who was and is the Creative word of God — that abideth at the center of consciousness in each and every one of us, *or* should one discount the words of Jesus — speaking as the Christ of God: "I will be with you always — even unto the end of the world". The Christ is none other than the "Lord God" or Dynamic phase of the Father Himself.

"Know ye not ye are the temple of the living God".

The thoughts I am transcribing here reflect the spirit of Jesus the Christ. They are in perfect accord with Universal Laws that never change from one Age to another and they represent the One True Standard that mankind must come to rely on for guidance.

A ship without a "reliable rudder", at the mercy of the sea, affords a very good example of the mind of a human being without a reliable Standard for guidance. How many times has the Master taught his flock in similar parables. It occurs that many, from the look of things, even after all these years, are unaware of the spiritual truths that lie hidden behind the Master's succinct parables.

I have mentioned heretofore that we are entering the Aquarian Age when mankind must renew its mind to meet the requirements of Reality. And again let me remind you that the Zodiac sign of Aquarius means "Water" and water translated, means thought or ideas.

Thoughts of the individual en masse mean "seas". When one comes across the term in their Scriptures and interprets its spiritual meaning, he or she will come into a light of understanding often very new and inspiring.

The cyclic, so-called Aquarian Age — "The Water Bearer" — symbolizes an age of "New Thought". Scriptures, speaking in parables, tell us we must be born again — not of the flesh, but of the Spirit. Speaking in parables again — was it not a cyclic age of advanced understanding (new thought) that saved Noah's ark from threatened disaster from the flood of mass negative thinking (seas) that preceded those times?

And, again, it was the cyclic age or *new understanding* that rolled back the negative sea of outmoded beliefs represented by the Egyptian's oppression — Moses was inspired by new understanding. He was encouraged by voices from the skies of his mind — but the Israelites were afraid because they found it hard not to believe in appearances.

Reading the spiritual message coming to us through the finding of those ancient scrolls on the shores of the Dead Sea plainly tells us it is high time mankind steps forward — not backward — in understanding what the Dead Sea (negative mass thinking) symbolizes.

Are you, the reader, able to look out upon all manifest nature and discern all as congealed ideas in the mind of

God, and pronounced good — as the Scriptures state in Genesis and support that concept with unwavering faith? Am I, the writer, going out on a limb to say that he is fast closing the gap in the ability to do just that? More than that — he unequivocally affirms metaphysics has taught him to see through an effect to the original cause.

Elsewhere in this treatise I have explained that the first manifestation of an idea is an atom and its indwelling idea is in essence — the Divine Creator. I have learned to mentally see the composition of all creation as pure congealed spirit. This is 'Reality' — this is 'Truth'. During spells of meditation I have found that nature can glow in spiritual Reality. I believe only through spiritual understanding in whatever degree one has come by is this possible.

The fundamental basis of spiritual understanding is love. The Master, Jesus, lamented the lack of it when standing before Jerusalem — "I would have mothered them as a hen her chicks, but they would not." That symbolizes the genuine Spiritual Love of God.

It is the collective erroneous thinking of individuals that is responsible for the breakdown of the moral fiber of our society today.

Trying to find a real remedy in this factual world of effects only adds up to more confusion, because the answer lies in the abstract era of First Cause. Our prisons are full of misinformed, misled human beings who have run afoul of laws made by other misinformed and misled human beings. In short, our courts base their convictions on factual evidence, not the causes that lie back of the facts. The 'renewing of the mind' voiced by Scripture must be the answer.

Recognizing and complying with the promptings of conscience, or giving Principle first consideration, leads us into a better and fuller appreciation and *understanding* control of the nature Physical Science has discovered, and thus a better and happier life for all.

The human and animal appetites are normal to physical nature but it must be controlled in the adulthood of man's higher purpose of existence. Otherwise it destroys the human individual in a thousand, mostly imperceptible, ways.

Psychosomatic disease, mental or physical, and the holocaust of war are among the most destructive effects. Though "Causes" may appear to be objective, they are always subjective. A metaphysical understanding of nature automatically reveals the cause, the effects, and the remedy.

The dawning in consciousness of the Truth is the "Savior" that comes stealing into the receptive awareness of mankind. All manifestation has its seasons. The procession of the Equinoxes symbolizes the ushering in and out of the ages in their due season on the wings of evolutionary progression. Today's Event — the "Aquarian Age" — signals the adulthood of man's consciousness, against a background of Eternal progress.

To resist progress physically, mentally or spiritually simply *delays* the destiny of the individual soul, whose purpose is fixed from the beginning — an expansion of the Creative Principle.

This treatise is an effort to condition the mind to the new order of concepts — not dogmatically by laying down rules, but by stimulating the thought processes of the individual. It is the individual who must discover his *real* self, for himself, through the reason and logic he is endowed with.

It has taken the writer a long time, as time is measured, to understand the truths as offered here, only because he started without formal education or really a serviceable equipment. This need not be a case nor a criterion held up to the reader. Rather it should be a challenge to his or her intelligence.

The key to answered prayer you have *always* had. Furthermore, everything you have ever had or will have, has come to you through the application of this key. Yes, though some are *totally* unaware of it — and some are *vaguely* aware of it — and yet, some are very conscious of it. The latter are the richest people in the world! They see no need of hoarding anything at all since it is as accessible as the turning of a key.

Jesus the Christ "had not a place to lay His head" — insofar as appearances go, yet, He could "turn water into wine", cause the blind to see, feed hundreds of people with a few loaves and fishes and He could speak the "Word" and bring to life the dead! Jesus told the people of that day, two thousand years ago, they, too, could do as much, and greater things. He was telling them then, of a key, a Divine key, that had to be *discerned* by the mind and that was not visible by physical sight. Also He told the people of that day not to do as He was doing but to do as He said! Only in so doing could anyone claim or prove the salvation He came to proclaim.

Yes, *the time* is the ever present *Now*, for when tomorrow arrives it will still be the *Eternal Now*. . . . And the place is where we stand today and tomorrow *unless* mankind comes to recognize the significance of that Universal Law of Progression. As it comes to me we will have more, not less, of the same.

Dr. Frank H. D. Buchman, initiator of the movement called "Moral Re-Armament", was stating this significant fact when he said: "People have been teaching the great truths in the wrong way. They lack the dominant passion to hear the plan that God has for their nations and the conviction to follow it. They lack the training that helps them to live for their nations and to re-make the world". The proof of Dr. Buchman's remarks lies spread out before the eyes of the world in terms of the effects of the perfectly adequate cause which he describes.

Quoting again from a speaker in one of the numerous M. R. A. conferences that are being held around the world — this time from the lips of Prime Minister U Nu of Burma. He said, in part: "More than anything else, the world needs to re-arm morally; I have continually urged my friends in other ideological blocks to rid themselves of fear and suspicion of each other. But when I have myself been beset with fears and suspicions, I realized how difficult it was for others to swallow the advice I had given them. So it is that certain things are very easy to preach but extremely difficult to practice. This is the big challenge to Moral Re-Armament."

So also, the writer is fully aware that it will be difficult for many to accept what at first glance may seem a cold, scientific approach to the understanding of the "God of Jacob". Here lies a challenge to the reason and logic that man has been endowed with — certainly to use!

In every sense of the word this book contains a message that is transcendentally important to the times, much of which was revealed inspirationally. It is authoritated by reason of years of concentrated and unrestricted effort to learn Universal Principles as distinguished from dogma of any kind. It is the *distilled essence of the letter of the Highest known Authority*. Concentration of the exploratory powers of the mind has resulted in the opening up of the faculty of the so called "sixth sense" of the writer to inspirational guidance — a faculty man has had from the beginning.

Many and manifold are the sources of detailed knowledge open to everyone concerning the subject matter of this treatise. In short, it is a work for those who have already traveled the "Textbook Path," and those who are intuitively ready for higher concepts of Reality.

There is one thing more that should be made clear to the reader before considering the fundamental questions herein involved:

The good to be found in every walk of life — the marvelously deep and meaningful charities along with those practiced selfishly or with strings attached or personal vanity — all, are good, relatively speaking. The spirit behind these actions is characteristic of the Age now in its transitional stage. The sincerity, of course, determines the merits of the case. In answer to a complaint that, "Some person was speaking in the Master's Name without authority," Jesus replied: "He that is not against me is for Me."

This treatise is not intended to be critical of any constructive activity whatever, which means it recognizes the lessons that must be learned through experience at the level of the Pisces Age. The Aquarian Classroom, so to speak, that civilization is now entering, has higher standards of conduct and a new language to fit these higher standards which must be learned.

There is no departure from the *Real or Spritual Christian Principles;* therefore, it is suggested the reader relax if it is felt there is such a departure. The author knows there is no discrepancy existing between the pure philosophy of the Christ and the Reality of Truth. *Jesus* was purported to have said Himself when He was called "Good Master", "Call Me not good; none are good but God." The language of the New Age deals in terms of Divine Law. And Jesus, when He made that statement was speaking as a human being and not from the standpoint of the Christ within Him which *is* God in man.

The contest between Principle and expediency in the mind of mankind, individually and collectively, has been going on since the beginning of time. It is perfectly normal. It is the way we grow in understanding. The masses, being made up of individuals, simply mutiply the contest. It is clearly evident that if there is to be a moral victory, it must take place first in individual consciousness.

Physical Science has progressed ever so swiftly since the beginning of the century. The atom merely existed as a theory fifty or sixty years ago, much less the inconceivable power it contained. Now we know for a certainty the center of even the infinitesimal atom is a nucleus charged with more power than the atom itself — a power that defies any physical means of measurement.

The cracking of the atom opens up vast new fields of scientific advancement in understanding the complexity of nature. Dr. Edward Teller, physicist of the University of California, says, among other things, that: "The mathematicians have given us new forms of logic." He could have gone much further and said: "What would the mathematician do without his abstract principle — the digit — "1" — What would anyone do without the name and principle of the imaginative 1st person "I" which we all express and multitudes never dream that in reality we are all speaking in the Father's name, but least of all, realize that He is the resident in the conscious life of us all without which we do not exist. Now if we couple the "I" with the "AM" we have the name of the "Lord God" or "Christ Principle" and the verb, "to be."

To create anything at all, we first have to picture it or *be it* in our imagniation first — and accept the truth that it is already launched into the creative process — then support it with our faith and patience.

Now we should see how the mathematician is using the same law without question to get correct answers to any problem he has. That is what *was* in the Scientist's *mind* when he made that statement.

There is another door of logic and reason yet to be opened, without which the picture is incomplete.

The geneticists have discovered the laws of inheritance. The chemists have discovered the structure of the crystals. Applied sciences have increased our observation of the planets in our own immediate Universe from a few thousand light-years to galaxies billions of light-years away.

And now, the physical exploration of outer space has been accomplished.

Without the releasing of the energy of the atom — which energy was here all the time — progress in this direction would be impossible. Without the opening of the above mentioned door — which subject this book deals with — physical science, as such, will be thwarted not only in its complete exploration of the nucleus of the atom, but the outer reaches of space as well. The unlimited energy of the nucleus of the atom as the unlimited space of the Cosmos, can be understood only through opening the door of metaphysical logic and reason. Can man hope to progress into the understanding of the Realities of life? Once that door is opened it can never be closed — and it must be opened — or the marvelous advances of science and technology will have been wasted on this generation. This is true even from the casual observation of facts.

The exemplifier of character is the moral principle inherent in every man from the beginning, however obscured it often appears to be. The realization and allegiance to this Principle, which we call "conscience," is a matter of moral education. It is an abstract quality generally opposed to any pull of the physical senses which ordinarily functions in the realm of physics. It is a lower stratum of the creative process.

The true purpose of the Christian Era is to introduce and prepare humanity for this incoming age of Aquarius when understanding thought becomes the standard through which the Divine Plan is carried forward.

"In the beginning," as related in the Bible, means the beginning of awareness in the individual. It is a well-known fact that the self-consciousness of the babe begins when it connects up in its mind, through its five physical senses (sight, hearing, taste, feeling and smell), a certain satisfaction afforded from contact with its mother's breast and hand. And from that time until its death its conscious life reflects on a rising scale, the report of its physical senses until it reaches the peak of its life span — old age; thence on a lesser scale until its spirit leaves the body, which, of course, returns to dust or the elements.

It is evident that individual thought-patterns are built up through habit. The continuous flow of impressions which we receive through all the outer channels of information, or the physical senses, weave inevitable chains that bind and tend to close the mind, causing it to resist the inner Source of Reason or our Judging Conscience, which is the most reliable. Only determined minds, insisting to know, will discover why it is that all observable nature from the microscopic amoeba we can see with a magnifying glass to the magnitude of the Cosmos is characterized by order and precision. Human beings will eventually learn about these deeper truths, you may be assured. I need not remind you that not by accident do human beings, the highest product of the manifest world, find themselves in confusion, insofar as Divine end — purposes are concerned — God's plan of Creation.

I believe that I have been given the reason, not to keep to myself, but to share. No doubt these thoughts are coming through to me to help you and me break the chains of habit — to make us think for ourselves — to use our God-given reason — not to accept or reject what I am saying here. Rather to prove, one way or another, through our own processes of logic and reason — the underlying causes behind the unquestionable off-balance of organized society. We are in the cusp — point of change — so to speak — of Cosmic Seasonal Change when adjustment must take place.

Who hasn't wondered where the outside of space ends — and what is beyond those limits? Physical Science has never even come near to the answer to that question. Only through the understanding of *Reality*, which is that all is spirit, can one come to know that there can never be a limit placed on the All in All nature of the Mind of God.

As these ideas come it is increasingly clear that the seeker for understanding and the solution of his or her personal problems or that of the world, shall never be found until the desire is stronger than the mental effort required to learn the truth. Everything in the world has its price and since this is a Universal Law, it must hold true in that which is to come.

I realize that everyone who reads these lines will not be ready for its message. However you may be assured, "When the disciple is ready the Master appears." The receptivity of the reader or his or her open-mindedness will always determine how well a message and its significance is absorbed and understood.

Mankind has existed the cyclic period of 35000 years which comprises the Pisces Age, under the dominant principle of Competition. Traditional teaching of many erroneous concepts of the *Reality* of the truths that the Master taught has resulted in stagnation rather than a dawning clarification of established Universal Laws — and this was a prophetic promise. As for example: We have worshipped in the dark until it has become a fixed attitude of mind; a refusal to accept one principle in particular — the principle of *Progress* in religious matters. Do you really understand how God could be man and man God — how He is Universal and at the same time be way off in the skies: How He could be the poor Medieval man and yet the Creator of all the universes? These questions I believe will be answered herein if the reader does not run too fast to really read.

There will be many who will have seen and understood before having read this treatise. For them the human materialistic foe will be partly vanquished already. Many will find themselves at the crossroads of decision. To choose is ever man's responsibility. To those who have religiously followed some orthodox dogma until it has *possessed them* or shackled their reason through habit and who, when reason began to ask questions, turned their mental backs and shut their intuitive eyes to inner promptings — to these, the message will be a disturbing challenge. All the force of individual and racial thinking will resist a "Light" that will be challenging at first. However, this reaction is perfectly normal. The farmer, seeing the "horseless carriage" for the first time said: "I don't believe it!" But he came to accept its developing benefits — after a time. The devastating impact of Hirohito's undeifying of himself was a blow to centuries-old beliefs. The thousands that have suffered death and the anguish and torment of the soul in mourning their lost dead, they too, are adjusting themselves to a new condition, though perhaps, in many instances, it may be a case of trading one superstition for another equally erroneous.

There is another type of partially developed mind that will rise in righteous indignation, "at first flush," with what they assume is sacreligious interpretations of the sacred Text-Book of the Christian philosophy — Often they will be able to quote the Scriptures from beginning to end. There is even division of opinion among the creeds as to which Book is the genuine and which is not. There are also those advanced souls "on the path" who will welcome the healing value of what these lines may have to offer. To these, the truisms contained herein will act as a supporting stimulant, for a sometimes hard-pressed faith, when they think of the senseless behavior on the part of some trusted servants of the body politic. To many, these fundamental Ideas will act as a combatting agent against disheartening experiences — disrupted plans, family divisions and other forms of disillusionment that beset society.

This message will also clear up many arresting questions regarding the meaning of obscure Bible passages. There will be those who will react like the lost "babes in the woods" yearning for some way out of deepening confusion — suddenly they will discover the warming sunlight of understanding-security.

The receptive mind of a child, in some way unbeknown to itself, recognizes the intrinsic nature of Divine Love, much easier, than the mind steeped in preconceived intellectual learning or the fixities of moral dogma. Years ago, my four-year-old son exclaimed, "She not sick no more, Daddy — she up!" as I picked him up so he could look for the last time at the still form of his ten-year-old sister as she lay in her casket. Should we debate the Source of the pearls of wisdom that fall from a child's lips? "He that hath seen Me has seen the Father." Surely we cannot doubt the Source nor the avenues whence wisdom comes.

Please do not accuse me of being presumptuous or dogmatizing but, rather, zealous to stimulate stagnant minds to weigh the evidence. None may ride into the mental state of heaven on the backs of another's belief or convictions.

For years as a child and in early youth I was overly objective in blaming my growing pains — the poverty — the hunger — or the inferiority complexes, on outward conditions. Never for one moment did I suspect or trace the cause to myself — to the pattern of my thoughts. I was embittered many times, and I kicked over the traces, as humans are wont to do, only to find myself in deeper water. The story of my own life is like the dreams we sometimes have — a racing after — a struggling to attain — or escape from, without quite enough of what it takes to accomplish the task. There came a time, however, that stands out in my life as the greatest milestone — when a great revealing light came "stealing into my consciousness," like in manner to the second coming of the Christ, which the "letter" of the Bible says it will be like. Finally I began to see a clear cut pattern of unfoldment that could not fit anyone but myself. From that day to this I bless the hard lessons that are now behind me.

One child in understanding will require gentle reprimanding in its erroneous behavior. Another will require stronger disciplinary measures. Still another will sit down with its parents or counselor and listen to reason. The psychoanalyst will pinpoint the psychological reasons for these differences in children or adults.

The innocent child or the ignorant tribesmen of the deep jungles of Africa are infinitely more receptive to truth than is the atheistic college man or the orthodoxically settled self-styled Christian. The child has no preconceived opinions — the atheist believes only what he sees and calls the phenomena "nature" and lets it go at that. The scientifically minded person believes only what the laboratory can test-prove of factual nature. Only after he proves his theory will he proclaim it a principle. The orthodox Christian accepts the theologian's version of the meaning of the Bible which often consists of an apparently symbolical hodge-podge of conflicting statements when read according to the letter. In this manner superstition is built up in the mind. The *Spirit* of the Bible is the *Truth* of it. Truth *never* contradicts Itself. Which is simply another way of saying, "Principle *cannot* contradict Itself." If it did, it could not be Principle. The contradiction, when there appears to be one, is clearly traceable to misinterpretation of the letter.

As has been said: "Everything has its price." The child pays for the love and care of its parents with obedience, helpfulness and cooperation, and reciprocating love which is the coin of that particular realm. Also, even the child withholding the price — to speak bluntly — "pays through the nose," eventually. "The Law plays no favorites." Justice may weep but it cannot violate the Law of its nature.

The ways and means for one to acquire understanding in

the category of physics, mathematics, science, sociology, art, philosophy, metaphysics or the Reality of Truth, will vary in individuals.

The dawning of *Spiritual Light* is not dependent upon how much knowledge has been gained in any lesser department of nature. Spiritual illumination stems directly from the Source of all Knowledge by means of the faculty of intuition or inspiration or the sixth sense. This is of course a well-known fact concerning the way the mind works. The greatest discoveries ever made come about through inspiration — though often accredited to outer causes. Reason was applied *after* the inception of inspirational light, *after* the idea was launched into the creative process.

Inventors are but souls with a purpose and highly developed sixth senses. The writer claims nothing so much as a developed intuitive faculty "paid for in the coin of the realm" in which it operates, namely: The Spiritual — the mental — and the physical departments of nature. The method used was continuous concentration on the subject with a will to know the meaning of life. I am convinced this desire was implanted in my mind for a purpose which was accompanied with a talent for it — There is intelligent purpose behind the delicate coloring of the orchid or the design of a snowflake. This is not the only talent with which it seems I am blessed. I have made my living in the commercial art field in former years, but philosophy superseded in later years because of its paramount importance in my mind. There is no such thing as accident in the light of the Principle of Cause and Effect. "Accident is a term covering up our inability to discern the Real Cause. It is unthinkable that there is a principle of caprice or of darkness. A child prodigy did not come into its intuitive knowledge by accident or in the brief span of this life.

Memory is an Eternal soul quality capable of development for, the soul is *cast* in eternity. It carries with it to each life's classroom what the soul has learned in former experiences. Those Eternal capacities could not be developed in one short semester. The more a soul is concerned with accomplishments that have only temporal value, the more certain is it to be found down the scale of spiritual development, notwithstanding its intellectual status. The Christian Bible tells us as much when it describes the characteristics of each of the twelve Disciples whom Jesus selected to follow Him.

Among them were ignorant fishermen — the whole group represented a cross section of the human race — individually and collectively. Individually the soul of man is likewise made up of twelve departments or faculties, undeveloped though they may be. Mankind as a whole is likewise divided into twelve classifications which, again like the individual, is evolving progressively toward the standard of completeness called the Christ of God. The great Emanuel Swedenborg said: "The human must be raised to a Divine status." It is said, "The poor will be with us always." Even today many people interpret this statement in an economic sense. Whereas the progressive evolvement of all segments of nature includes the understanding of Reality from the shadowy concept (the poor) to a progressively greater knowledge of the individual's relationship to creation and the laws which govern the "Creative Process."

What is needed is not so much a matter of more churches, as such, but more ministers who will recognize all the departments of nature and wed them in a common unity to the *spirit* of the Christian philosophy, as opposed to the letter of our Bibles — and what is more, teach it! Why the Christian philosophy? Because the spirit of it has proved itself absolutely scientific. The question of Principle versus expediency is a serious matter. This is not to say that many ministers do not, in lucid moments, rise above the habits of dogma into the calm quiet thought-waters of inspirational meditation, and realize the discrepancy between the letter and the spirit.

As I stated above — the Spiritual basis of the Christian philosophy, as I have found it, is absolutely scientific. There is no place for conjecture, superstition or contradiction. Its guiding principle is Cooperation, ("to jointly work together for the same end") not competition (or "survival of the fittest") — not cancellation of the animal law which has its own lawful department in nature — but to rise out of it and fulfill the purpose for which the soul of man was created — *that* Principle in whose image man was created in reality, does not compete with Itself.

Do I hear objections from those whom the chains of habit have formed fixities of belief? Those who have fallen victims to dogmatizing superstitions that fix patterns of thought — that make static that which is meant to be progressive? Whoever you are, please do not be offended — I am merely passing on that which has come to me and which has proved to me both reasonable and scientific. Even as I write, the lights — the ideas — flow into my mind in never-ending volume. This fact, too, is explained in the Bible in many places. Does it not say: "Seek ye the truth and the truth shall set you free?" (Free of wanting, free of error). *Wanting* something, even mentally, is a confession we do not have whatever it is we want. I suggest you read the 23rd Psalm again — "Thou shalt not want." "Knock, and it shall be opened unto you," (the doors of inspirational guidance). "Come unto *Me* all ye that are heavy ladened and *I* shall give you rest."

We must become or possess the things we want in mind, first — this, of course, implies faith.

No one can escape the purpose of their calling. The seekers that are alert are those that will be raised first from darkness into light, "at the first trump" — or what conditions and remembering the Principle and what we as a whole people are doing about it, is it not clear we are trying to match our wits with the *unlimited* Eternal Laws of existence, with but a *limited* vision of what Truth or Reality is?

There is a taboo in the publishing circles against controversial subjects mainly because it is considered unprofitable. For the *same* reason the churches deliver to the people outmoded ideas they doubt themselves. It is the sugar-coated — wrapped-around popular but mysterious verbiage — made more palatable with a sprinkling of quotations from famous personalities, presumably authorities, pertaining to the subject. These are the things that publishers reach for — themes that have been subjected to and passed by the censorship of an insecure and face-saving clergy and their adherents.

The clergy was scolded in Jesus' time and the spirit of the mob that crucified the Master, Jesus, is in our midst today! Intolerable of progressive new concepts, as in those days. That mob was not composed of a degenerate class, but the very ones who confessed to the same God in their material temples but rejected Him in the holy temple in which Jesus said He reigns supreme; namely, deep within our conscious selves. If this isn't true, what was Jesus talking about when He said, "Know ye not, ye are the temple of the *living God?*" And again, "He that worships God in spirit and Truth shall see the kingdom of heaven."

Nobody has a corner on Truth, but the really free mind will give at least a hearing to the most unpromising of theories. The free mind will accept on *approval only*, any theory however scientific or not it may seem to be. That is the way human beings are lifted up and out of ignorance. What is acceptable today may prove unacceptable tomorrow. But tomorrow, when it arrives, will still be today. And so again the Bible says: "Now is the propitious time" — the Eternal Now is the only time we have in consciousness to enjoy or suffer. To sit down and settle on one theory, be it true or false, without putting it through the acid test of those well known Eternal Principles, is not using the reason with which man is endowed.

Listen in on the discussions of the experts in every department of the natural world of physics, science and technology and we will find a deafening silence in the direction of Eternal Spiritual and Metaphysical Laws. Yet in this realm is to be found the *real* cause and the *real* answer to the personal and general problems facing civilization today.

Mankind is plainly out of balance with the main purpose of the creative process; namely, "progress" — it is characteristic of the vehicle through which the Father extends Himself in creation; namely, the finite mind of man. Here again is a valid argument why reason cannot accept stagnation in the matter of spiritual progress — no more than in the category of Physical Science. Is there any wonder Science has reached a position far in advance of the moral forces that should pace it? How can the juggling of *effects* ever head off the rational method of salvation? Selfishness is a by-product of ignorance of the law of our Being. The animal is excused because he has not arrived in evolution to a self-conscious entity. But the souls of we human beings have. Along with this arrival, we assume responsibility, whether we want it or not. "A chain is no stronger than its weakest link." If the links of human values are lacking in understanding, which is the strongest ingredient they possess, the whole civilization will break down in the fires generated by friction, which in turn is brought about by selfish competition and resistance to change, which again has been given rise through lack of the moral adulthood of understanding. And finally, to those whose great responsibility it is to teach true principles. However, this backtracking does not stop with the teachers, but at the individual's receptive or unreceptive mental level. Freedom of choice is mandatory. Whichever way we choose draws its pay. Only the blind fail to see this great truth. Socrates was thinking of this Principle when he said, "Kings should be Philosophers and Philosophers, Kings." And the "Hemlock" *proved* his allegiance to Principle.

In so-called free nations the leaders are chosen by the people. The standard of the morals of the leaders will depend upon the standard of the majority of their thinking constituents, as will be their intellectual aptitude, which, of course, is important, but not of the first importance. Physical Science is also important but not of first importance as is now being brought out by its headlong flight out of control. Again this message is for the closing of the ranks — the amalgamation of all departments — the marriage of Science, via Metaphysics, to Religion when religion means Truth.

The time to put out a fire is when smoke is discovered. In the case at point it begins with the overhauling of the educational systems — physical, mental and moral. This must be accomplished, of course, by first inducing a favorable mental climate in society — by implementing emergency use of every channel of education open to mankind. The burden and character of this initial educational drive must be *the Truth according to known Universal Principles*, "no punches barred" because of race prejudices. The pressure will be on making people use their own reason and logic and not dogmatizing any segment of the multitudinous beliefs at the expense of another except as it is found wanting in the scope of Truth.

The greatest need plainly shows up in the moral and religious departments of society, as it is reflected in the product of our educational systems. This is the citadel of error that balks the great white Light of Truth it is supposed to teach, and not the realm of physical science, as such. An awareness of the wrong use of the fruits of Physical Science's Technology is becoming increasingly evident in the minds of thinking people everywhere. Councils and groups are debating as never before in the wake of public resentment. The search is desperate — yet, and tragically, the solution is so close that it is overlooked. Mystifying dogma must be stripped from the Truth man was created to know. The Church and the State, which are the people in the last analysis, must be made ready to look within the citadel's walls for weaknesses they seek outside of it.

The writer appears to be commissioned to write this treatise, shocking or not, because of an all-powerful light he must share. There are many doing the same thing. Some will receive the Truth in one manner and some in another. The vibratory power of the Word of Truth is high — the combined force of many speaking the same Truth will shatter the walls of the "citadel of error." What the effects of this appeal will be remains to be seen. All I can say is: My direct lines of communication have never been working so well nor flooded with so many lights bearing upon the most critical times of this Age. It is my feeling that nothing short of a shock wave of Transcendental Metaphysical Truths injected into the channels of education can shake the minds of thinking people out of their deep complacence.

Christian Principles have stood the test of the centuries. Principles that contradict themselves are not Principles at all, but mere theory. A sacrifice imputed to God is error and cannot be proved. It is tantamount to saying God made a mistake. God *is* Principle and Principle "changes not" — and God *is all*. To hold that God had to sacrifice any part of His Being to save another part is pure unadulterated fantasy that still persists today in the orthodox churches. Clinging to the superstitions of ancient doctrines on the face of it is not progressive, and who will not agree that *progress* is a Universal Principle of life. It is the very opposite to "stagnation" which we know to be "death" — not to Life, for Life can never die — it only changes its vehicle of expression.

The writer believes this message will conclusively prove this metaphysical fact, if the reader will consider this book with an open mind.

Chapter II

WHAT ARE OUR STANDARDS?

Are they based upon Secondary Causes or First Causes? Are they based upon standards established by accepted scientific experts of the effects or factual side of nature?

Can one really understand "Cause and Effect" short of exploring the abstract side of nature? Are not factual causes forever in a state of flux — forever shifting to meet the onward, progressive march of technology?

Are not the textbooks of colleges based upon someone's authority or facts established by someone who, in turn, has come by his knowledge of the facts of the material world — not the realm of First Cause — and again, from someone accredited with authority in his day.

The passage of time has proven time and again their standards were faulty. Are there any psychological, material or factual conditions, of whatever nature, existing in this world of effects that did not have its inception first in thought?

Can anyone be conscious of anything, in any other way, other than thought? These questions back right up to First Cause.

There is no compelling power that is forcing us to think destructively or constructively. Mankind, again, has freedom of choice. But our deep indwelling convictions are, by Universal Divine Law, outpicturing in the world about us.

Saint or sinner is not excused from penalty or reward, not by a prejudiced Principle, but by his own misuse of the laws of Being. We suffer because of our ignorance of Spiritual Reality. If our standards are based upon factual reality — quoting Scripture again, "Judge not from appearances" — they are, on the face of it, unreliable.

One cannot be sure of his moral position in life, much less the real relationship he has with the world of matter — or shall we say, our thinking stance in life on this plane. There has been no inner change of my deepmost convictions regarding the progressive process of a soul's objective — namely, perfection in the Divine Plan.

Whether the reader is a deeply conditioned religionist — "the man of the street" or "a so-called atheist", if he or she will listen open-mindedly to the deep-down dictates of the soul's conscience, a light of truth will be coming forthwith.

Until one has tested his convictions with trustworthy standards he is hardly in a position to deride a proposition he does not understand. This is the earmark of closed-mindedness, which is another name for unprogressive ignorance.

In the old days there were parents who fought off school teachers coming into a district where there had been no schools. Things have changed because of the progress we cannot deny.

Of course progress can be negative and towards destruction or, on the other hand, towards the *balance that must be* the nature of our Divine Creator.

The writer can never cease to marvel at his own physical body that has survived 88 years of his life — "This time around." I believe I have had my share of miraculous *escapes or healings*, which ever way one might see them. At this moment I consider these experiences as blessings, though I have called them dozens of times, "just dumb luck."

The real answer is "progression" under *true Standards of Reality*.

THE CHRISTIAN ERA

We cannot truly be Christians and at the same time carelessly violate the Spirit of the Master's teaching.

Look to the Spirit of the "Lord-God" that teaches: "I will be with you always" — Where? Again.

At the very center of our consciousness. That is where our thoughts come from. Your reason will confirm this truth. This is the place in the "Skies" of Mind to look for the "second coming" of mankind's Savior — That is the location of our conscience, which is trying to guide us right.

Do you want to learn more about what is needed to correct the course of our *uncivilized-civilization?*

If you do, may I suggest: Do not stop here because of perhaps "unfamiliar territory." But "listen," and be encouraged to direct your sincere questions to that dynamic phase of the Father Himself who said: "I will be with you always, even unto the end of the world" — not way off in the Skies but where our Savior has said He would be: — When speaking as the Christ of God.

Yes, through Metaphysics I have come to *understand the truth that sets us free* — and *that* is open to all mankind when they are ready for it.

I love the discernment that the Metaphysical way of thinking affords.

There are many Religious Philosophies in the world but few that have really moved out of the superstitional tradition of the letter of their Text Books. The degree, the spirit of any teaching, that cannot align with Universal Standard Law, on the face of it, is a negative influence on mankind.

From a comparative standpoint, *only from observation alone* — the impact *of well-being upon the people* — *Christianity* must rank the most constructive.

We have but to look what has, and still is, happening around the world today. Factual happenings speak loud and clear for a Metaphysical rebirth of mankind's evaluation of the Realities of Life. As it comes to me — there is no other constructive alternative.

There is a great awakening to problems of Ecology — The careless and destructive pollution of our forests, streams and lakes and the destroying of the wild life. All, when seen in the right perspective, adds up to Ignorance of the Truth of life and why these blessings our Divine Creator has placed *here for us* — His co-Creators in God's plan of Creativity — what else — not for useless suffering!

Is there any wonder the Master Jesus is pictured as a sober and sorrowful person looking upon the ignorant behavior of the people and even in His last moments said: "Father, forgive them, for they know not what they do."

I watched a most graphic portrayal of the evolution of man on T. V. the other evening — produced by "National Geographic," titled, "Time of Man" — going back hundreds of thousands of years — centuries that are but fleeting moments in the time and space of Eternity, before the advent of Man. Cycle after cycle of evolutionary progression was portrayed here, coming right up to the present day.

The illustrated picture of the destruction of mankind's environment constituted one of the most powerful endorsements of my plea for "Metaphysical Understanding" — the type of understanding King Solomon of the Scriptures truly voiced 2000 years ago.

The 36,000-year cycle I have mentioned heretofore is but a brief period in the generation of even our own planet as I have pictured, symbolically, herein. Even briefer periods are symbolized by the 12 signs of the Zodiac — all symbolic conceptions.

It is evident that past generations had reached a remarkable degree of understanding — as witness the building of the ancient pyramids of Egypt which, even today, are puzzling the scientific minds of our times.

While we are dealing with legendary symbols of what has been accepted as factual — let it be said: "I, too, have accepted someone else's ideas on approval pending 'inspirational guidance,' which has proven to me the most reliable. And this guidance truly comes from a spiritual Source nearer than our very breath — "Our Conscience" at the center of our consciousness.

Millions of devoted religious people are still seeking a kingdom of heaven way off in the skies of the "Hereafter." — Yet the Master Jesus, through the media of Scripture, told the people of His day that the Kingdom of Heaven is within us.

Now let us turn briefly to what I like to think of as the ABC's of the ancient symbols of the creative process.

(Please turn to page 183.)

In the diagram — "A" represents the Divine Life Principle or "I". The letter "F" refers to the large circle representing the Infinite awareness of Divine Intelligence.

The small circles "B" represent the limits of *individual awareness*.

The cross bars "C" that intersect the Divine center of the Life Principle "A", stand for the *Divine Creative Word* or the dynamic phase of the "Father of Lights" (God) which the Scriptures call, "The Christ of God."

Note, that the *large circle* of Divine awareness "F" runs through the intervening bars "C" of the small circles which is indicative of the dynamic creative power mankind is endowed with — in the *"Name of the Father,* or "I AM:

(the verb to be). This makes mankind responsible for what his thought-ideas create — Always in the Name of the Father. (Like the imaginary principle of mathematics, the digit ("I")).

When we use either Principle correctly, we get right answers — yet, they are mental concepts — symbols that are metaphysically in tune with spiritual Reality. Note: The Encyclopedia refers to the term Metaphysics as meaning: The study of the science of "First Principles" — above and beyond the physical being of the *essential nature of "Reality."*

To me, this has come to be a tremendous simplification of the complexity of nature — an *understanding relationship* the souls of mankind have to their Creator.

Now, since the dynamic phase of God, or Divine Intelligence, is also present at the center of each and every individual of mankind with his or her field of awareness as represented by the smaller circles "B", just as the larger circle "F" indicates God's field of awareness extends to infinity and at the same time *links up all* the individual circles of awareness of mankind — for, in reality, *"We are all One in God."* The symbolic diagram proves this point throughout the whole process.

Divine Principle is in perfect balance — until "It" moves to create something. Then It moves through It's dynamic phase. Variously called the "Word of God — The Christ of God" — "The Lord God" which I have explained elsewhere. This Spiritual Presence indwells us all, and again, at the very center of our consciousness — in particular at a point between the two lobes of our brains — where our thoughts come from. — Where else?

The cross bars "C" represent the Dynamic phase of the creativity of our Divine Father. Scripture plainly points out that all things are created through the *"Word* of God" that indwells us all. And again, let us be reminded, every thing we attract to ourselves we do so in the Father's Name "I AM." It should be constructive but it can be destructive — It's our choice!

In your study of the six stages of the Creative Process — remember "A" always stands for "Diety," which has two phases: "I", (Static Substance) and "I AM", the dynamic phase, which the *man-idea* must pass through while in human form. The Spiritual souls of us are cast in Eternity and (as I have noted elsewhere) must learn the guidelines of Divine Law in many "classrooms" of human experience. And this, I may add, he is unconscious of at the time. One comes to this knowledge through practice of the Principles.

When one realizes that an idea once launched into the creative process will manifest in exact accordance with the degree of "faith and works" support that it gets — positive or negative — and this by the workings of the Universal Law of Cause and Effect, that leaves no alternatives.

Most people understand and respect universal laws but millions do not, as witness the adherence to substandards throughout even the organized society of our times. In the diagram — The 1st day circle represents the static idea of man in the mind of the Divine Principle before it is launched into being, the "Alpha" or beginning. The 2nd day circle represents the 1st movement of the creative process. The "cross bars" that intersect "A" are indicative of the *dynamic movement phase* — the Christ Word or Lord God. The imaginative building phase is represented as a gaseous condition enclosed in the circle of awareness. It is the beginning of the atomic structure which is basic to all creation. A detailed study of the symbols of the Creative Process will be taken up later in Chapter VIII.

THE ADVANCE OF SCIENCE AND TECHNOLOGY

The mountains of wonderful products we see all about us are mute evidence of the advancing strides Science-motivated Technology is taking. Standing still in this department of creation is understood to mean death — not because the writer or anyone else believes it, but because of the underlying *principle of progress*. This eternal evolutionary principle is not confined to any one of the departments of life known as the Physical, Metaphysical and Spiritual or moral phases of the Trinity.

This, as former generations read ancient history, and except for the few who have lived and seen the changes in the past 30 to 75 or 85 years, takes the marvelous fruits of progress pretty much for granted.

The moral and stabilizing checkmate of the Christian philosophy has lost its effect simply because it sets itself apart from the laws governing material progress. It goes on blindly singing the non-productive song: "The old time religion is good enough for me" — as though *religion* was a synonym of Reality!

The man in the street is a cross section of civilization. He represents every walk of life. The time and thought he devotes to the moral issues of life are but a fraction of that which occupies his thoughts during a work day. He generally will be found in the offices of the seats of government, industry, the laboratories of science, education, and the trades on the production end. A large portion will be found directly or indirectly occupied in the category of National Defense. His preoccupations pertain mostly to social enjoyment. It is clear why the greatest progress is made in these above categories. Also, it will be seen why civilization is off-balance — why science, technology and the appetites for social and physical satisfaction are in the vanguard of advancement.

The most important fact of all that must be brought out here is the stagnation of that stabilizing moral we call principle, "Progress" which by law, not sentiment, turns the end purpose of science and technology for the most part to constructive rather than destructive effects. It is said: There is hope even "unto the eleventh hour" — for the receptive mind or minds. Through science and technology have come the beautiful church edifices of our day but the spirit on the inside of these edifices has changed comparatively little since the "darker" ages. On the human scale, a home may be a castle but far from being a "home" without the moral spirit. Does it seem so far fetched to say: A human intellect may be a giant in relation to its fellows but, fact though it be, his gifts — his talents or his accomplishments could and often do cover an inner darkness.

Some of our foremost scientists have moments when they seriously question the use their skill and knowledge is being put to — the moral promptings of their heart do not jibe with the popular concept of what is right and what is wrong. They would rebel more if they were to extend the energy they use in exploring the field of their calling to include metaphysical philosophy. As it is, they themselves dictate the limits of their activities. They are content, perhaps, to leave to those whose talents seem to make them best qualified to investigate the abstract — besides, their instruments of measurement are only standard in the realm of physics, — let alone the fact, the *terms they use* are incompatible to metaphysics. This is not true with the practitioners of metaphysics. In this department of nature their explorations merge into the spiritual, moral and physical equations as naturally and frictionless as night merges into day.

Understanding may be far advanced in any one or two of the three departments of nature but it takes an understanding of all three to even approach a knowledge of their relationship to one another.

Physical Science has broken down the elemental units of composition as far as the human body is concerned. But the inherent Life principle baffles their ingenuity. If Physical Science were as particular in their acceptance of authority in the category of Spiritual and Metaphysical understanding as they are in their own department, there would be a much closer balance in human affairs — a much happier civilization.

To the majority of citizens, reaching for the moon is more important than understanding the power that placed the moon where it is and why. If the light reaching earth from a star hundreds of light-years out in space is on a curve, that curve must be the arc of a circle, or the law of numbers is not a law at all! And if this is true, then what must be the condition beyond the procession of the equinoxes? The answer does not lie in the realm of Physics.

Let us consider briefly the significance of our Solar Orb as symbolized on page 184 imaginatively, when we backtrack a single ray of the sun from its end purpose in nature, we will find we are lead to the Source of Light — the White Light — the Mind of God which indwells the center of the sun as it does every planet in space or every unit-atom in Creation.

Backtracking the extreme of heat leads one to the extreme of coldness — or complete balance, i.e., no vibratory movement. Like the digit of mathematics — static until our mind dynamically uses it for some purpose. Or again, like Divine Mind activates Itself through the Dynamic Phase of Its Being — the Lord God or the Christ Principle.

When we transpose the meaning into Biblical terms or the 'Triangle of Being' — the Father, the Son and the Holy Spirit (Ghost) all are one in Divine Mind. There can be no separation, only in Its purposeful function in creation. We cannot see physically the resolving of the multiple colors of the color spectrum into 'pure white' but we know it is true. Metaphysics teaches us to discern the truth of any apparent mystery. We may pass our entire life's classroom in fluxuating laws of physics and all of its variations and still be blind to the first cause of every effect in factual nature.

As has been said, "The poor will be with us always." If it were not for the law of Progression they no doubt would remain so. The living of life on the plane of effects is a continual challenge. Hopefully, the reader will meet the challenge he or she is faced with herein — for it does challenge traditional acceptances.

CHAPTER III

THE TRIANGLE OF CREATIVE PROCESS
SPIRITUAL - MENTAL - PHYSICAL

Whether we seek understanding studying from a material base or a spiritual premise we are faced with the necessity of metaphysical equations. We cannot acquire reliability in our beliefs and convictions any other way, simply because we have been endowed with reason and freedom to choose what we believe.

Imagination is the mental faculty of abstract discernment, as the eyes are the physical instruments of sight on the physical plane. It requires imagination to grasp an idea or mental light whether motivated from within by way of inspiration or from without by way of physical sight or the less gross psychic faculty or animal instinct. The conscious mind of man is the "circuit-breaker" of the eternal process of creation. "Metaphysics" is the name given to the study of the conscious mind's position in relation to the other two points of the Triangle; namely, the spiritual and physical nature of creation. To imaginative Metaphysics must go the credit of learning and therefore progress on every plane.

Throughout the Ages, with increasing regularity, are those who wanted genuine illumination strongly enough that they were willing to pay the price. The price is mental concentration held by the will in silent meditation upon the subjective mysteries of creation.

The Master Jesus demonstrated "the Way, as well as the Truth and the Life" and He also, through parables, showed how each and everyone receives his penalty or reward, not by a capricious God but by a Just, Divine Law. The same principle, commonly known as "Cause and Effect," operates on every plane and in every department of nature.

The purpose of this chapter is to show how metaphysics is the determining factor of just how much or how little the soul of a man is abreast of a real understanding of the laws of creation — and not to describe in particular the step by step pathway from the conception of an idea to its fulfillment in manifestation.

The great emancipating "Way Shower" said in one instance: "No man cometh unto the Father except by Me." Orthodoxy has interpreted the meaning of this saying as: Belief in the man, Jesus, as being a Divine personality. Metaphysics interprets this scripture as: The Christ of God or the Word of God or that which not only abided in the man Jesus, but abides in "every man that cometh into the world," which Jesus said, when speaking as the Christ; "would be with us unto the end of the world." Christ is Divine. When Jesus the human became one with Christ *in spirit* He became Divine in spirit and His body reflected that fact. As did the power of His word.

He who keeps the "Commandments" is one who permits his conscience to dictate his thoughts and actions. Until one is ready to read the Holy Bible metaphysically, he is among the *"poor"* whom Jesus said, "would be with us *always.*" This truism bespeaks: The Divine Principle of Progression. Until the student is ready he is not receptive to instructions of a higher order. Swedenborg taught that a soul in the "hereafter" was not barred from any of the heavenly grades — but the light was too bright for comfort in those grades higher than his own; and likewise, the lower grades held no interest but a great desire to get out of them. Metaphysics makes sense to the statement "the poor would be with us always." The implication of the "letter" of the Bible contradicts a heaven where the poor is unknown. A man may be in a mental state of heaven, yet not blind to those that are poor spiritually, mentally and physically.

Solomon said: "With all thy getting, get understanding." One does not acquire understanding without progress. This fact is evident in every department of nature. All nature is embraced in the nature of God. Yet Spirit, the very essence of nature, is still being held in captivity to old, old superstitions. This is not progress and progress is the basic element of the creative process.

Metaphysics teaches that in reality there is no such thing as a miracle — but that "miracles" are the resultant effects of the working of Universal Laws that are misunderstood.

Understanding and the unification of the three departments of creation — spiritual, mental and physical, is to be signally accomplished in this New Age of Light. These departments have been symbolically referred to as the "Trinity" — the three points of the symbolical triangle. Variously interpreted as, first, "I", *the Father*, which is static: second, "I am", *the Son*, which is dynamic: third, the Reflecting Soul, *Holy*, when made so by practice of the principle — Otherwise, what we see with our physical eyes is merely a reflection of the Soul's understanding; a garment for use on the physical plane. (As a man thinketh deeply, so he is, as is his world — in *his* individual consciousness). Every thought or word the Soul thinks deeply "becomes flesh" and manifests automatically — for he thinks in the first person ("I Am") which is the name of the Father in action. It will be seen, metaphysically, that man creates his own heaven or hell in the Eternal Now. Jesus knew this and taught it. Jesus said: "What so ever ye ask *in my name, believing* shall be granted." Jesus did not promise what we got would always be to our liking. Our destiny is a matter that was and is settled from the *soul's* inception — not the human's birth into this material plane. The purpose of the souls of men which were created in the image of our Father, in potentiality, is to carry out and multiply the Divine Creativeness — an eternal neverending *"process."* As the Father doeth, so likewise His Image. Nothing in this Universe of Universes is static except the Divine Principle signified by "I".

The mystical coming of the Saviour in this new Aquarian Age (Age of Thought) is *metaphysically true*, but *mystical* to millions upon millions of religious people of this globe. But the coming Saviour is a dawning in our individual and collective minds of Truth — the Truth of the soul's real relationship to God — a realization that the innermost God (The Christ) has always been our life but which through ignorance we have persistently refused to acknowledge — looking and praying to a God outside for help and guidance; Sadly, it is the mystifying dogmatic superstition of the Ages and has held man's natural disposition to progress in religious matters in chains — hence the moral side of nature has lagged far behind the scientific or progressive side of nature, which it should pace and guide as an individual and collective conscience. Hence, we perceive civilization is out of balance with the evident purposes of God.

The metaphysical Christ which we may call the "Wayshowing Principle" and which is That inner Intelligence, is responsible for the activation of our reason. It has been referred to for centuries as the light (Christ) "that lighteth every man that cometh into the world." However, the meaning has been obscured through mystifying and confusing dogma. We have been told of a mystical coming of the Saviour. Millions even in this day believe this coming of "the Bridegroom" will take place in the sky. Metaphysics interprets these parables as an awakening in the minds of men and women to a brilliant truth concerning the creative process and the individual's relative position in the scheme of things. The unifying Principle, variously called "the Bridegroom" — "the Christ within" — "the Way-Shower" — which conveys this new knowledge to the conscious mind (when it is receptive) is none other than the "second coming" of the *real* "Saviour" which has been with us as Principle always, but until this Age, few have been able to realize it (or make it real). It is the One and Only metaphysical principle called, "The Word of God" — through which and in Whose Name ("I") all things come into "being."

Those who are ready will understand this message and those who are not ready will come to understand in due time. The time, as I have said before, will depend upon how urgent our desire, how the individual exercises his mind and reason to know the Truth.

Orthodox beliefs have shied away from metaphysical interpretations of the Christian Text Book as though it were poison, stigmatizing the term, "Metaphysics" and confusing it with the term, "Modern" which reflects, so it is believed, a sacreligious un-Godly world.

The truth is, the development of the metaphysical phase of the creative process has uncovered the mystery and superstition that has hidden the real meaning that underlies the letter of Christian principles. It is to metaphysics, which I believe is the real Saviour, that must go the credit for making sense out of many conflicting statements which, in common parlance, we call "double talk." Orthodox theology, itself, has not uncovered the inconsistencies of the letter of the Bible, and when Physical Science reaches the end of the usefulness of slide rules and laboratory test tubes it, too, must give way to the realm of metaphysics. Abstract equations must be arrived at mentally. Physical Science is as yet unprepared to accept "1st causes" arrived at through spiritual discernment, yet the very ideas that set their laboratory mechanism to work were abstract theories, at the outset of their investigations. The Source of all ideas is abstract and comes from One Spiritual Source.

Physics is connected with metaphysics and metaphysics resolves itself into the realm of Spiritual Cause; hence the meaning in the sub-title of this chapter — "Spiritual-Mental-Physical." The *application* of *science* without a true moral rudder is like a ship in a tumultuous sea — the sea reveals its dangerous hidden rock formations only on the occasion of an extreme commotion. The Bible has a name for this situation, too: "Man's extremity is God's opportunity." Only when the going gets tough does man reach out for something beyond his comprehension.

The churches are filling up now with those who have a fear of catastrophe — they are those who have let their church attendance lag because of *doubt in their hearts* concerning the adequacy of what the church was teaching — and not because of an unbelief in God.

I say again, mankind must assess its religious moral principles through the portals of metaphysics. Our God is not a capricious God but a God of Law, "who casts no shadow of turning."

"All nature is the body of God." Therefore, every particle of it is God. Logic and reason tells us God does not have to ask for anything. He already *is!*

We have but to extend the *truth of Reality* a little farther and realize (make real) that man, made in the image and likeness of God, creates everything in his consciousness by *willing it to be* or not to be, which is in both cases, the same Law. In order to make this all-important point clear, I have used many angles of explanation, all of which sums up to the same thing: namely, a general need of metaphysical understanding, to appreciate the wonderful destiny in store for mankind. Yes, as the Bible indicates, it is a gift, but it must be earned "by the sweat of the brow" before it can be accepted. "The sweat of the brow" means the work of concentration of thought on the subject of wisdom. This mental activity *is* "work." "Grace" is the Divine power given us to use — just as electricity is given us freely to use. This, as will be seen, brings one to the study of the meaning of life, or metaphysics.

The fall of man is the same as saying there is no such thing as a law of evolution or that man, i.e., the soul of man, is not under the Law of his Creator in whose image he is made.

A child born into a human family may have all the potentialities of his parents but he has to learn, and learning is primarily a mental activity and mental activity is the expenditure of energy and the concentration of energy generates heat; concentrated heat generates physical light — concentrated physical light brings one to the threshold of our Spiritual "Father of Lights." Light is understanding. In its higher forms it is wisdom. Again, it must be clear, man earns his right "to sit at the right hand of the Father" — to represent and create in the Father's Name. The necessary gift to man was "freedom of choice," otherwise, the stature of the Father could never be approached, much less gained.

The stature of the Father is the stature of the Christ, Who is one with God. The only begotten of the Father — the Dynamic phase of the Father — the Word of God through which all things come into being and without which no thing was made that is made.

Gaining the stature of the Christ is not usurping His

power or His position but becoming a clear reflection or image. The human being will perform as he perceives the inner Christ counsels — the Christ performs as His Father God dictates. With all, we have the significance of the Trinity: The Father, the Son and the Holy Spirit.

Man could never occupy the position he does as a self-conscious thinking individual outside the laws of God.

A wise man is he who understands the nature of Universal laws and applies them *constructively* — which implies they also may be applied *destructively*.

THE WARNING APPROACH OF THE NEW ERA

Metaphysics ushers in the bright "New Day" — a sign of the "second coming of an awareness in the minds of men — a consciousness of their relationship to the "Creative Principle" — an understanding of First Cause of which man is but an effect.

Philosophy warns of the approach — Metaphysics, the actual arrival. *A brilliant conscious knowingness takes possession of the mind of those who are ready.*

Metaphysics is the rationalizing principle that makes sense to the reasoning faculties when material means of measurement lose their usefulness in the face of higher phases of nature — the supernatural — but still, nature.

Metaphysics deals with abstract ideas from their inception through the period of gestation and development preceeding manifestation — *the nebulose of imagination.* It is in this area that many ideas lose their way in the purpose of their calling. Simply because the instrumentality (the mind of the soul of man with its tool, the brain) has not *realized, not merely thought about,* that once an idea arrives from its Source and is in consciousness, it is already in the *creative process* and must be supported by faith (conviction) through the gestation period until the idea is *born* into manifestation where the physical senses will then support, through factual observation, that which they could not while it was in the abstract phase of creation.

There is no thing or condition that ever appeared or is psychologically sensed that did not or could have arrived in any other way or through any other channel. In metaphysics there is no such a thing as a miracle. Inability to trace an effect to its underlying cause is not an assurance that an accident or miracle has taken place. The Voodo witch doctor and his "black magic" — the Indian "soothsayer" or a legitimate occulist, though miracles they appear to perform, are all without exception under the law of *"Cause and Effect."*

If a universal principle is *really* a principle it can never be anything less. Once in this space and time world men believed, without a shadow of doubt, that everything that went up must come down — that was before they discovered the world was round, or found a way to overcome gravity — and before they realized "up" and "down" are merely relative terms. When man finds his physical way to a globe in outer space he will find the principle of gravity has not changed in any way, but attracting him up insofar as earth is concerned, and down in relation to the planet he is seeking to land on. Not to mention the reversal that appears to occur if the observer is standing on the opposite side of our own earth. The magnetic power exerted is, of course, mathematically determined by Principle.

Metaphysics traces all ideas to what the Bible has termed the "Father of Lights"; also, that an idea in the mind is really a light in the imagination. A comparatively new discovery of physical science is that *all things are resolvable into pure vibration which evidently emanates from the center of our Solar Orb; and that the rate or frequency*

of vibratory impulses varies in material substances.
Metaphysics takes these factual discoveries and "back tracks" them through the formative nebula of imagination to their vibratory Source — "The White Light of Truth" — "Divine Substance" — to the All in All Mind of "The Father of Lights".

Man must learn not to obstruct God and His justice. In simple terms, the billions of rays of the sun are vibratory rays that emanate from the center of the sun outward to all nature — without which manifest nature could not exist. But the sun itself is but an instrumentality — not the Source. The rate of vibratory impulses in *all nature names* or identifies the segment *by number.* No two things have identical purposes or numbers. As the color of an object is determined by its rate of vibration which reaches the interpretative mind of man (which is but a segment of God-Mind) by way of and through the instrumentality of the eye and brain, likewise is the relative position of any created thing or condition or purposes identified.

From the slow, cold inanimate forms of nature to higher and still higher rates of vibration — through friction — heat — fire and physical light, thence through the psychological and metaphysical path of discernment (as distinguished from physical sight) until it reaches the Principle of Light — which is not only the Source or beginning of Creation but the ending as well: thus, metaphysics supports the spiritual version of the Holy Bible which says: "I Am the Alpha and Omega" (the beginning and the end). Mind creates and supports that which It creates through a polarity existing between Mind and matter.

Pure metaphysics discerns the principle or "Father of Lights" or the "I" which is *"Static Intelligence"* — in the identical way the principle of mathematics — the digit "1" is static until it is used. There is no limit to the extent the digit can be used or how long or how short the period of its usefulness.

Metaphysics also clears up, or in common phraseology, "makes sense" of the term "I Am". In metaphysical terms, it is the dynamic force or power of will to know — or the activating phase of Divine Intelligence. It is the verb "to be" — the opposite of wanting. The principle of mathematics can never deliver a desired sum unless put to use.

If the mind of man can conceive an idea and focus on it with all the power of his will it is possible of accomplishment. The creative forces of the Almighty has in its storehouse of knowledge the ways and the means to any end It chooses. Again the reader is reminded, Principle is not limited.

Scientists at this moment are bending every effort to place in orbit a platform from which they plan to concentrate the rays of the Solar Orb to any location they choose. The implications are the changing of the climatic conditions of any area by controlling the weather; melting the polar caps — iced-in harbors — or raising or lowering the temperatures to desirable or devastating levels — burning one section to a crisp or introducing another Ice Age. This is not an alarmist statement.

We have already witnessed some first phases of these possibilities. Like the principle of mathematics, man may use this power for good or evil. Will he choose in the spirit of competition, and defeat his selfish ends, or embrace the moral principle and direct these transcendent powers to God's purpose which includes all mankind without prejudice? In the strictest sense of the word — man may use Infinite power but he can not exclusively possess it!

The principle of mathematics is an abstract concept in mind (imagination) but we cannot escape from its use if we want an answer to a mathematical problem. So, abstract or not, we accept its dictates and prove that it is principle by using it.

We see the effects of electricity, but not electricity itself. We prove the principle of life (the Father of Lights) by its effects. We see Life and Intelligence looking out of each other's eyes and we finally come to realize that everything we experience in life comes to us in the Father's name, "I", yet the *human eye* has never seen God — only discerned Him in imagination. Therefore — denying the metaphysical approach to an understanding of Truth is like refusing to cross the only bridge that leads to succor from a forest fire.

If the Israelites had listened to their fears, generated by what their physical senses reported, and not the counsel of Moses, or the voice "in the clouds," they could never have crossed the "Red Sea" into the "Promised Land." Moses was a type of Christ — the inner Principle that counseled him. Metaphysics is the Bridge that every soul must eventually take before he or she can clearly reflect the unshadowed image of the Creator. Oh, yes, human beings are "children of God" but a child has to learn eventually to think as an adult.

CHAPTER IV

LOOKING WITH THE IMPUNITY OF UNDERSTANDING

To a spiritually alert person, the warning approach of a climaxing phase in the order of events is like the dim distant rumble of an unmistakable approach of a clash of the elements.

Effects are, of course, always the inevitable result of an adequate cause. That, I believe, is widely understood! Significantly, today's news headlines tell us of the greatest floodings in the history of the United States taking place right now in many Eastern states. The thought comes to me that perhaps there is a deeper meaning — a deeper cause than that blamed to the hurricane spawned off the Atlantic Seaboard.

As I have noted elsewhere, the symbolical meaning of 'water' in the letter of our Bible means 'thought' and 'seas', mass thought. I have a deep feeling, as many others of like mind, that a great wave of new thought is taking place around the world.

Are we looking with understanding when we glance at the news headlines or television for just one day's happenings in what we like to consider a civilized society? The sad side of the picture is that it is of our own making — especially since it need not be! God, the Father of Creation, has given us all, that indwelling creative Christ Principle, plus freedom to choose how and for what we desire to bring forth into our lives.

We cannot point an accusing finger at something we call 'the establishment' for we are all included in this pace-setting generation. Under this situation, sooner or later, unrest must break out — or there isn't a Divine Law called 'Cause and Effect'. Severity of the trails the world must endure as an effect of our own making is in exact ratio to the resistance set up to spiritual progression. That is the essence of the message of this book.

Let everyone focus their attention on this truism and place themselves in relation thereto if they would learn something of the underlying causes of world unrest — for religious movements, by reason of their importance in the shaping of morality in the individual — consequently the mass — it must follow, when error exists in their interpretation of the Spirit of Reality which Jesus taught that of necessity must align with Universal Laws as they are known to be today and as they ever have been. Is it not clear where much of the responsibility rests for the negative trend in civilization's deterioration so threateningly immanent?

The writer realizes that to some, these statements represent a challenge. However, with complacency, in the face of what is taking place in our generation, he is at a loss to reconcile his convictions not lightly arrived at. If it be comforting let me say my guiding support rests with the Spirit of the Master, Jesus', teaching of Divine Laws — and they are eternal.

I believe it was Shakespeare that gave us his far-seeing views in the following:

"Our remedies in ourselves do lie,
Which we ascribe to heaven".

And Walter Malone shows how to approach an error

and correct it, in a verse of his poem: "The Law of Supply."
> "Wail not for precious chances passed away,
> Weep not for golden ages on the wane!
> Each night I burn the records of the day —
> At sunrise every soul is born again!"

Emerson knew whereof he spoke when he said:

> "The soul answers, never by words,
> But by the thing itself".

It is very easy to misinterpret the meaning of Emerson's vision of Principle if one overlooks the fact that the *Real* part of *anything* is the *spirit* of it.

> "He who seeks wisdom will assuredly be taught,
> But thorns of fate have thorny thoughts behind,
> For out of our own hearts our lives are wrought" —

said some unknown Poet.

If it is true that "Each desire implanted in our mind bears its own harvest, after its own kind," then, it must be equally true the harvest the world is reaping today is the answer to negative prayer. And if this be the cause the world is surely in need of a "Shock Treatment"! The term "world", in the sense of the context, is All Inclusive. It follows as night the day, the ones that need it most will, of course, get the brunt of it. And the ones who already see the light, will be thankful — and spared. These few personalities above, whom I quote, have chosen to be in line with Truth, but, there are many who have not had the vision. However, as the Scripture states: "They, too, have their reward."

The formula and key to answered prayer is as always, "Believing". The Creative Principle is forever being that which *it wills to be*: not wanting something it already has.

Its will says, "Let there be". The stumbling block that resists believing something is the inability of the physical senses to see things that are hidden during the gestation period which all creation passes through. A new and higher understanding removes the stumbling block because it reveals the mystery of that phase of the Creative Process that is hidden from physical observation.

It is important to note here the Principle enunciated in the well-known Bible quotation, "When ye pray for a thing believe that ye receive it and ye shall have it," is still as true as it ever was. For "believing" that one has already received something is not wanting something by any stretch of the imagination, but *having it!* — The Twenty Third Psalm.

The support and clarification of this higher concept of the eternal Truth is plentiful in Christian philosophy; as for instance, "Forgive us our debts as we forgive our debtors — or as we *first* forgive our debtors. We therefore *become* that which we desire — in this case our desire is "forgiveness." So again, the "Creative Word" is the word of "Being," ordered by the conscious will and not the world of *wanting!*

For emphasis let me say again: "The Word of God *is* the Word of Being." Remember, the Bible says, "In the beginning was the Word and the Word was *with* God and the Word *was* God." The old concept of prayer is, "Lord, *if* it be Thy will, give us this or that"! But Jesus said plainly, "It is the Father's good pleasure to give you the kingdom" so there are no ifs or buts about it! When we carry out the rules which call for *being* in our imagination first, whatever it is we desire, our prayers are automatically answered.

The inability to accept is simply a matter of lack of knowledge: *knowledge* is a derivative of an *understanding* of the Creative Process and *how* the mind works in conjunction thereto.

Whichever way our prayers have been or ever will be answered is always in exact ratio to the confidence in the Truth of the statement: "Know ye not ye are gods," or "Be still and *know* "*I Am God,*" or "Ask whatsoever ye will, in *My Name, believing,* and it shall be granted unto you." A formula so simple, millions miss the grace of it.

THE MERGING CUSP OF CHANGE

The differences that exist in the language of the oncoming 'Pisces Age' and that of the present 'Aquarius Age' is one of degree. Aquarius stands for the 'water bearer' (new thought). Over the centuries comes the Master's prediction of a time when there would be a renewing of the Spirit of Truth — a 'second coming' in the heavens of the minds of mankind. That time is at hand. Tradition's name for it, according to the letter of the Scriptures, was 'new birth'.

The culminating 'Pisces Age' that follows is the 'flowering' time of Spiritual understanding — the meaning of 'Love'— the nature of God, in whose image the souls of mankind are fashioned. The Christian era of the past was when Jesus taught a new commandment to 'Love thy neighbor as thyself' and that kind of love was the fulfilling of the Law.

This is the time when survival of the fittest, 'the animal law', must give way for the higher spiritual law which is to dominate the hearts and souls of mankind. Today the bookstands are full of self-help books written by those with the marvelous talents for making themselves understood. They are all good when they lead one in the direction of higher understanding. The Master Teacher taught 'Spiritual Truths' not generally cognized by the five physical senses. These are the 'truths' that are coming into general understanding. The approaches to this new light are varied. The one that has served the writer best is called metaphysics. I presume the writer is just another instrumentality bringing a higher concept of Divine Law — at least to some who will listen with open minds. Knowledge of the spiritual truths are sometimes harder for formally educated people to accept, but those of the younger generation are reaching for more satisfying answers. It is this 'due time' when they will come to know the reasons our society is failing to stop the trend towards self-destruction.

LIMITATIONS OF TRADITIONAL RELIGIONS

Speaking in terms of the Christian philosophy — has it ever occurred to the reader that there is something amiss when we read of the characteristics of Jesus and the principles He stood for and try to reconcile those principles to the teaching and practices of the Orthodox Christian Church in whose name it professes to teach? Does not the Bible say — "The letter killeth but the Spirit giveth Life"?

Let us consider in this chapter some of the contradictions found between the letter of principle and principle itself — principles which are so common that they go without notice or comment. Yet, basically, this is the flaw that has been and is now, more than ever, responsible for the lack of spiritual progress in relation to the advance of physical science and technology. In other words, the 'letter' often hides the underlying meaning of an intrinsic truth.

Intolerance in religion is bigotry, a byproduct of dogmatism often based upon the traditional letter. It is seldom recognized at the time by the person afflicted — only after progress is made in understanding is there a change of heart. An unbiased teacher doesn't condemn or criticize a child because of its inability to readily grasp a new and higher principle of that which he has been studying. But what about the teacher? Is he as receptive as the child?

An authority in the category of any department of education is one who has earned the appellation through study and test-proving theories for himself. An authority in the ecclesiastic dogma has supposedly earned his vestments. He may have studied the letter of Scripture to where he perhaps can quote the Bible from end to end. He may be zealous and meticulous for exact quotations of the letter — yes, this is his earned right to authority, insofar as it goes. Divine Intelligence used many facets of His Infinite Mind to write the Bible. It is to be presumed that the instrumentalities chosen for such a monumental task had come to understand thier responsibility. But this does not guarantee that interpreters of it thoroughly understand the full significance of what they read. The hierarchy of the church in that day when Jesus was crucified, evidently did not understand it or they would not have done what they did. And let us not forget, the mob followed their lead!

General understanding of the underlying spirit of the Bible in those days cannot be compared to the understanding existing today, or evolutionary progress is a myth and this is unthinkable, if only in light of the progress made in every other department of nature.

The negative and positive facts are: While the constituted authorities of ancient dogma are still teaching in accordance with the interpretations of a dead past, a new generation of teachers has and are rising fast to meet the requirements of the New Age of Light and Reason.

It should be obvious that, unless one lays aside preconceived beliefs and opinions, at least long enough for serious consideration of broader and higher consideration of broader and higher concepts, he lays himself open to the label of intolerance and all the term implies. The Master, Jesus, counseled against the attitude of hardheaded assumption when he voiced this Scripture: "Except ye become as little children ye can in nowise enter the kingdom of God."

If Divine Intelligence is both love and justice, there can be but one rule that applies to the order of His universe. Special consideration for any individual or group cannot hold with proven principles. Cause must ever be in strict relation to effect and vice versa.

The churches of all ages have been built on the letter of their particular dogma. The power it exerts and perhaps enjoys over its adherents is implemented through the mystifying of the Truth or Spirit of the Principle it is called to teach. The natural outgrowth of this procedure is, through force of habit, to bind the mind to error. Our Scripture says of this: 'Whatsoever ye shall bind on earth, bind ye also in heaven.' At the very outset this must be seen as contrary to the Spirit, in particular, to the Christian philosophy. I quote again from the sayings of the Master: "I came that ye shall have life more abundantly" — not to mention that which is of the highest importance and which the quotation implies: namely, an understanding of the nature of all departments of life, which, again, necessarily begins with *progress*. Stagnation always results in death or as our Bible puts it — "The letter killeth but the Spirit giveth life."

As we have noted elsewhere, science and technology is away out front in the matter of progress — so far, in fact, that it has lost touch with the spiritually-moral (not materially-moral) stabilizing factor which should pace it and which again, is a matter of development of character.

The rules of the church, like the rules upon which our Government or any responsible organization are set up, form the basis of organizational principles, in order to better facilitate and extend the services or purpose of its being — which clearly *should be* a better life for all society. Ordinarily, when we speak of the City, State and

National Governments we refer to the economic and social well-being of society and the peaceful co-existence with its neighbors on the *human* level. When we speak of the church, we speak of an organization that deals with, or should deal particularly with, the instruction of the people in the ethical and moral values which should *guide and shape* the purposes to which the fruits of man's progressive efforts should be assigned.

If the church fails to understand or obey the higher Divine laws it is called to teach, which basically is spiritual progress, leaving unstabilized the progressive ingenuity natural to man, then it must be clear the church is performing a disservice that has far-reaching percussions — as witness the uses the aforementioned scientific ingenuity is being put in this hour.

I have just read a report of the F.B.I. wherein it states: "Crime has nearly doubled in the past year among teenagers, which now accounts for nearly half of the criminal infractions of the law of the land." This alone should give us pause to reflect what is wrong with our moral development — remembering, to youth must go the task and future responsibility of moral government.

Reason accompanies the action and success of every development. Reason and logic is not an exclusive faculty. All normal and semi-normal minds are endowed in greater or lesser degree with this faculty. When the church teaches traditional superstition and conceals known principles in mystery, they are not only down-grading the quality and purpose of the God-endowed faculty of logic and reason, inherent in man from the beginning, but they restrict him in the necessary exercise of the above-mentioned faculty. To follow the lead of ancient practice is stagnation, not progress.

Man is entering the age of his adulthood — something must give! No man or woman is bereft of instincts and the faculty of inspiration. No minister of the Gospel is without misgivings, at times, concerning the ethics of his preachments. The very gap in the progress of science vs. religion should be sufficient to cause at least great misgivings, if not a courageous step to close this gap in the interest of greater harmony with the self-evident laws of life.

The effort to bring about a universal church has not been successful because there exists an erroneously fostered competitive spirit — whereas, Truth is another name for a non-competitive God, or Principle. This fact must carry sufficient conviction in the hearts and minds of church leaders *first* before success in this direction can be accomplished. What reasons other than *outer* reasons can the church reject what their own conscience must counsel? Conscience is the seat of inspirational guidance — this is fundamental to all spiritual progress.

The scales are heavily off-balance in the councils of men weighing the destiny of our civilization. 95% of the debating time allotted to solving world problems — which always find their way down to the individual level — is concerned with the physical aspects or effects and not with the abstract Causes. The roots of the problem, in every category, are on the unseen side of nature. The more pruning of the outgrowth, the more widespread the problem becomes. The roots lie on the abstract plane and are best approached metaphysically.

Sanctimonious-sackcloth withdrawing from normal life is *running away*, not facing the lesson the individual soul must learn for himself. Life is dynamic and creative. Creativeness entails outer action in the society of mankind and in the physical nature which he surmounts — simply because it springs from the activity of thought.

"Faith without works is dead." The power of a Father confessor cannot lift the responsibility from the individual soul of man. He can do no more than point the way. And if he points away from Truth, knowingly, he is an imposter. If he is blind himself — what availeth his leadership? If he does not take to heart the spirit of Jesus' sayings: "The Kingdom of Heaven is within you," and *"When ye pray,* withdraw your thoughts from the outer world of man and things of effects to the center of your consciousness where the *living* Lord thy God is ever present in His Heaven waiting for recognition", — what is it but a case of "blind leading the blind and both fall into the ditch"?

We are counseled to "Be still and know that I Am God." Let your attention fall again upon the eternal Truth, namely: God is life — Life is One — and when you speak the Creative Word, you speak in the Father's name — "I", or in the First Person, the Son or the Christ of God.

Can you reconcile the 'lowly Jesus' who could command the sea to be still — the dead to live — the blind to see — the cripple to take up his bed and walk — yet 'not a place to lay His head'? And who said, "Know ye not ye are the Temple of the Living God?" With the grandiose material temples that are built with hands and in some cases fabulous glittering vestments of the clergy — the rituals and glamour-wrapped symbols supposedly representing the man, Jesus, who was born in a manger but who, speaking from the standpoint of the Christ within Him, said He was appointed from the Father to rule — mind you, not in a material world — not in Caesar's world, but in the 'Kingdom' not of this world. It is where the pattern is made that eventually 'becomes flesh' in accordance with man's ability to read the pattern.

As all must know, Jesus' power was spiritual power — the power to command all material wealth if need be. He knew there was no need to hoard anything for any purpose whatsoever. The treasures the Bible speaks of are not material but spiritual. They are to be laid up in the heavens of the soul — they consist of the 'Knowledge of Universal Principles'. This knowledge goes with the soul as part and parcel of it, and no man comes by it but by being or living the Law. Nothing can take it away — much less the mere transition of the soul from the material body.

Was it Jesus' spiritual power that influenced His followers, or the miracle raising of the dead — or the feeding of the five thousand — or the restoring of sight to the blind — or the walking on the water? Are there no souls living on earth today who can perform such things by reason of advanced spiritual power? Are the Divine Laws of today any different than they were in Biblical times? If the principle of progression is not any different today than when Jesus walked the earth — why do we not see such miracles happening in these times? Or are we to to assume they are parables that are to be interpreted spiritually along with all the letter of our Bibles. Instantaneous healing, to the writer's mind, must take place within the Divine Laws of Mind — not the limited ability of eyesight to cognize what goes on behind the scene. Or again, 'Cause and Effect' as a Universal Law has no validity.

The treasures that are made so much of in this material world are of but temporal value — even these treasures cannot be fully enjoyed without understanding their nature. Scripture tells us: "The poor shall inherit the earth", — Real wealth is not earthly, but spiritual and eternal, whereas material wealth is transitory. The poor in understanding are poor in spiritual wealth. The philosopher's body, no less than the body of Jesus, has its seasons. It wears out, so to speak; however, a better way of putting it and much nearer the truth is that it, too, becomes no longer of use to the soul. To go a step further, it can be said that the Father's purpose behind the soul simply takes a step forward in evolution when the soul leaves the body.

The body, a temporary mechanism, may wear out but the mind of the soul still gyrates in accordance with the soul's position on the evolutionary pathway. Death is unknown to Life and Life is God and the soul partakes of It. So, whence comes death? Like the non-existent devil, it is a figment of the imagination that can become so vivid that humans subscribe all the power they can muster to it, and paradoxically, always in the name of the Father. People make their lives subjective slaves to a mere belief — fostered by erroneous appearances. I suggest the reader think the answer out for his or herself!

On our coins we read, "In God we trust." What percentage gets the most trust: the allegiance the motto enunciates or the coin upon which the inscription appears? Again, to the reader must come the answer.

Morality is preached in the churches, but radio — T. V. — magazines — newspapers — motion pictures — theatres — night-clubs — and in the so called exemplary homes of the intellectuals, the pendulum swings far and away from the principles of Christianity. Who will deny that from these sources thought-patterns get their form?

Money has been erroneously called the "life blood" of our economy, but in fact, and in truth, money is a poor representative for the spirit of progressive and productive industry, which is the real life blood of the economy of any state. It is generally believed that removing the money incentive removes the industrial interest. However, our best scientists reflect a different story. Again, there are millions creating the world's products who receive but a pittance by way of monetary gain, yet happier than those with large incomes. It isn't that money is evil except it is used selfishly. It is a commodity the same as the goods and services it represents. When used to facilitate the economy it is a genuine service. However, merely giving lip service to the underlying purpose of money brings us back again to moral issues of life.

Sooner or later a people falling prey to the temptations money presents find themselves in trouble. They lose touch with Principle, for they find, through force of habit, their thinking revolves around monetary gain. There is a principle that says: "To him that hath shall be given and to him that hath not, even that which he hath shall be taken from him." A man becomes materially rich or spiritually poor by the same law. This may sound like a reversal but it is not. To he that is poor in spirit, as applied to anything, loses what he has — simply because lack in mind begets lack in expression. Here again we see the working out in our everyday life, the principle of Cause and Effect. Another saying comes to mind that supports this truth: it runs like this, "To each his own." So, "As a man thinks in his heart (or deeply), so is he." It follows then, that "like attracts like." Did anyone ever hear of an effect without a corresponding cause?

To non-progressive moral doctrines must go the burden of responsibility for an off-balance society. The symbol of error and falsehood is adequately depicted by an *upsidedown* spiral. The point of the apex represents the seemingly insignificant falsehood very easily, but precariously, balanced as a base at first. However, as the spiral rises, coinciding with each turn, it increases its weight and scope until there comes a time when the whole collapses of its own weight — Its sins have caught up with it — "with bang"! — so to say. Can you, the reader find any good reason why this is not happening to civilization today?

"NEGATIVE THOUGHT" — THE DESTROYER

Negative thought over which only man has freedom of choice, destroys the human individual as the negative collective or mass-thought destroys Civilizations, as is shown even by recorded history. Besides, the evidences are plentiful in the discoveries of archeologists. Bearing out the fact that long before the letter of Scripture described the advent of the first man, Adam, many civilizations had sunk in the abyss of the *negative use of the eternal law of cause and effect.*

There is no point in detailing the everyday accounts of mounting local crime as it reflects itself in national and international tension the world around. The aim of this message is evidently to show where the roots of the trouble lie.

The human animal thinks in terms of "survival of the fittest." Noah, and the Ark he was told from within to build, is a fitting illustration of the result of negative thinking. Note, in the story a pair of every creature, including man, was saved. And note again, the animal as well as mankind, suffered the same fate — with the exception of Noah, who listened to God — the "Inner Knower."

The metaphysical interpretation of this first civilization after Adam, so the story goes, was destroyed by water — or "a flood of negative mass-thought." The destruction of the present civilization, the same Bible prophesies, will be by fire. And except for Divine intervention (or new Divine concept to millions) the destruction would be complete. Metaphysical understanding points up the truth, which is, that those who take the trouble to understand the nature of all departments of creation and the laws governing them, rather than an outmoded dogmatic interpretation of life, that has been handed down from an Age of immaturity, will be those who will be protected from harm. Which again points up the significance of the prophecy where it tells of the "first fruits being caught up in the skies" — meaning the skies of thought.

It takes water to put out fire. Fire is generated by friction; friction is caused by contact of opposing forces, and thought is force. Destruction overtakes those that resist the march of evolutionary progress. This law of unfoldment is inevitable on all planes, including the moral or spiritual plane.

The New Age is not *accidentally* called the Aquarian Age. As the Creative Principle adheres in the telescopic cosmos or the microscopic molecule, so must it adhere in the evolvement of the human soul.

On the grand scale it can be likened to the "Procession of the Equinoxes." On the individual scale we may trace the evolutionary cycles that develop physical man from the lowly amoeba to the physical organism called man. It is comparatively easy to trace man's development, from the so-called Adam phase or the advent of the first self-conscious human-being, through his half-animal way of thinking, which coincides with the Age of Competitive domination; until he arrives at adulthood and merges with the superseding higher plane of Cooperation which in turn, corresponds with the Aquarian Age — the Age of thought of Creative Principle — the Father's domain of Cause. The significance of "the return of the Prodigal Son" is apparent.

The story of the "fall of man" does not suggest an error. Rather, it tells, symbolically, of an eternal process of Law wherein Principle, through evolutionary law, creates the qualified agent, man, through regular channels common to all creation.

Chapter V

UNIVERSAL LAW VERSUS TRADITIONAL SUPERSTITION

Metaphysics has been accused of many things — mostly by powerfully entrenched orthodoxy. There must be a reason why!

To prove a case against a theory is a comparatively simple matter. But to prove a principle false one must have solid irrefutable grounds for the accusation. There is no room for bias or personal opinion, much less superstition or theory in such an attempt.

Colton, famous English clergyman of the 17th and 18th centuries, is quoted widely today as an authority on ecclesiastic matters and I think the following quotation illustrates an untenable position which is held by much of the religious world. Colton complained: "Metaphysicians have been learning their lessons for the last 4,000 years and it is high time they should begin to teach us something. Can the tribe inform us why all the operations of the mind are carried on with undiminished strength and activity in dreams, except judgment, which alone is suspended and dormant?"

Metaphysicians have never or could ever claim to have all the answers for Metaphysics, as such, is a pursuit, not an end of knowledge! However, as to dreams: Some of them result from various stimuli arising from such as an excess of mental occupation during consciousness — fears;

frustrations; suspicions; premonitions; fright; physical hungers, nutritional or sex. Then, there are those that arise from mental and physical illnesses or temporary irritations while asleep.

Answers to significant dreams, when sought by the conscious mind in the first few moments on awakening, come quite readily to those whose sixth sense is developed to any great extent. As has been said before in this book, all understanding arrives by way of ideas that come into the mind where it is then subjected to reason and logic. The writer has had many experiences that attest these facts. As an example, I relate one of them here: I am or was a heavy man — some 220 pounds. Every time during the night I'd weary of lying on my right side and half consciously roll over on my left side for relief, resulting in slumber again. However, I will also invariably have frustration dreams on these occasions. This type of dream, of course, is physically motivated. My heart struggles under restricted conditions; I awake perspiring and with great relief to find whatever it was I was trying to escape from, or catch up with, or perhaps lose, was only a dream!

Here is another type of vivid dream I had, just three days after my wife had passed on: I was sitting in the living room in my favorite occasional chair, reading. I thought I was alone. I was finding it difficult to concentrate on the book for my mind insisted on being concerned with my bereavement. I detected a movement or a presence other than myself in the room. It seemed to come from across the room in front of me. The room was not overly light for it was late in the afternoon. As I looked at the back of a figure standing before me and dusting off one of my canvases, I realized it was my beloved but deceased wife, Georgette. There she stood as real as in life. The thought flashed through my mind that the vision was but a dream for Georgette had been gone three days. I quickly took in the circumstances and my mind wanted to make the most of this extraordinary experience. I exclaimed, "Georgette!", half expecting the vision to fade away. "Won't you speak to me? Can you come back?" As I spoke I got up and walked up behind her. I wanted to put my hand on her shoulder and gently turn her around but I was afraid it would spoil everything. But Georgette, as if she read my thoughts, turned slowly and faced me. Her face wore a wistful smile. I was impressed with the appearance of years that had in some way disappeared. She had lost at least fifteen of her apparent years. But my Georgette only smiled back at me and slowly turned away and walked toward a door leading into the kitchen. I followed her. To the right of the door, in the kitchen, hung a mirror. Georgette turned toward that mirror and started to dust it off, as she had the canvas. The thought occurred to me as I came through the door, if I see her perfect reflection in the mirror I'll know for sure whether or not she is really here. I peered over her shoulder and there, was her perfect reflection! That was too much for me! I cried out, "Georgette!" That outburst of pent-up emotions awakened me.

There I lay with nothing but the realization that I had experienced a terrific dream — but nothing else. As I lay pondering the question of life after death, dreams and related subjects, the passage of a book I had read recently came to mind. The gist of it was: "Often in bereavements the mourned loved ones would return in three days — either in a vision or in a dream." I got out of bed immediately and went to the book shelf and took from it Harold Shermond's book, "You Live After Death" — and this I'll never forget: — I opened the book and without turning a page, there before my eyes was that identical paragraph! Now, I feel the above first-hand authentic experience answers Colton's question in at least, some small degree. I hope he has changed his opinions!

Cecil, another so-called English divine who lived in the same 17th and 18th centuries, and who was adamant to progress and impatient of change, said: "Metaphysicians can unsettle things but they cannot erect anything. They can pull down a church but they cannot build a hovel."

Cecil, like Colton, had yet to discover the trouble was in their own unreceptivity to change. They squared everything according to their own and the church's limited tenets, much of which were and are baseless and unprovable in practice despite the realms of intellectual verbiage wrapped around the purported linking of their authority to ancient traditions — ancient beginnings of the trail. One might well ask who, living today, witnessed first-hand those ancient beginnings? Short of known Universal principles, what *has* anyone, to support their claims?

Except for actual proof of tested Universal laws, Metaphysics would have little meaning for the writer. And this is not mere syllogism.

As to Cecil's accusation: The answer as I see it is, Metaphysics deals with a church *"not built with hands."* Rather, a temple erected deep down in our hearts. The adherents of a material church who are most interested in the things "Caesar's world" and its pursuits and material trappings can hardly be said to be completely devoted to things of the spirit. Did the "Master Builder" indicate the corner stone of His church was material? Were the highways and byways where He taught, any particular church? — If only to speak in terms of Christianity. And as to abilities — I think we must agree, one's greatest potential lies where his heart is.

Intellectuality, when it gets out of hand, more often than not, attempts to usurp the position of Wisdom. Voluminous and highly intellectual works are written around competitive Bibles. The layman searching for a religion that conforms to reason, gives in to one or another of the multitudinous denominations; usually the one that appears to offer the broadest shoulders to lean on, the greatest service to vanity, pride and prestige — the greatest show of intellectual knowledge — the greatest assurance in whose hands they can trust their spiritual welfare. So, the church with its particular interpretations does their thinking for them. Yet, in the face of Divine Reality the responsibility forever lies with each individual soul entity.

There will always be divisions of opinion, but never division of Universal Law. The following quotations from so-called authorities that lived in the past indicate how true it is, despite the fact that some have braved the breaking of traditional thinking, to which the many still cling.

The French poet and dramatist, Francois Marie de Voltaire, (16th-17th centuries) thought great in his day, nevertheless, showed little understanding of true Metaphysics when he said: "When he that speaks and to whom he speaks, neither of them understand what is meant — that is Metaphysics, understood, is based on known Universal Law and not hearsay or superstition."

Now here in the following, is a breath of fresh air, from the pen of Aldous Huxley, the illustrious English author: (1894) "It is in the light of our *beliefs* about the ultimate nature of *Reality* that we formulate our conceptions of what is right and wrong, that we frame our conduct." It will be seen that the responsibility for the correct interpretation of Principles lies with the teachers — whatever they teach, believing or not, they plant into the receptive minds of their hearers. It is like planting a seed that parleys into endless fruits, fruits that can mean misery and suffering or happiness and security.

Real vision is expressed in the following two quotations: "Metaphysics is the anatomy of the soul." So said Jean de Boufflers, poet and French Marquis (1738-1815). And again: "Algebra is the metaphysics of mathematics," by

Sterne, English clergyman and humorist. (1783-1868). Both of these men were speaking with their feet on solid ground. Both acknowledged the abstract was fully applicable to what is Spirit, as well as to what is called material — both were speaking of provable ideas — both had a knowledge of Metaphysics in an advanced degree for their times. I quote again, "Metaphysics are whetstones, on which to sharpen dull intellects," writes Henry Ward Beecher. But the way the writer is given to see it, Metaphysics holds much more profound significance. Who it was that expressed the following isn't clear, but it fits the writer's attitude very well: "If your adversary be ignorant, instruct him. If he reasons erringly, detect his fallacies. But against ingenuity which you cannot equal, or demonstration which you cannot disprove, do not, if you would respect yourselves, cry out metaphysics!"

Therefore, to reduce to an axiom — Metaphysics is a pursuit — not an end in itself. But *Creation* is both an end and a process. The only discovered motivator is *thought* — Divine *Thought*, working through Its own creation, on the level of that particular creation's position in eternal progression. This, then, *is* Metaphysics, and not superstition, whether traditional or not.

The list of modern luminaries is long and growing longer fast — but not as long, by far, as those still teaching untenable interpretations of Reality. The latter, it will be noted, draw much the greater following — it is so much easier to fall on one's knees and arise a Christian! Then, besides, trying to find one's way is really a strenuous experience for most mentalities. So, one goes drifting along riding the tide — one time on the crest of the wave and the next in the trough.

We attract what we *are* in our *convictions*, shade for shade — and not one tittle more, or less. One may not have a dollar to his name but be rich in mind and the reverse is just as true, though he had a million. It is also true that millions will answer this statement something like this: "Just give me the million dollars and I'll consider the philosophic question later."

The poet, Hadji Abdu-El-Uezdi grasped the significance of Jesus' message:

> "How then shall man so order life
> That when his tale of years is told,
> Like sated guest he wend his way;
> How shall his even tenor hold?
>
> "Be true to Nature and Thyself;
> Fame or disfame court nor fear;
> Enough to face the still small voice
> That thunders in thine inner ear.
>
> "Spurn every idol others raise,
> Burn incense to thine own ideal;
> To seek the true to glad the heart,
> Such is of life the Higher Law,
> Whose difference is man's degree,
> The Man of Gold, The Man of Straw."

Speaking from experience, if the reader is one of these, I suggest he or she "stop, look and listen," for to heed might well turn out to be the most priceless milestone in their lives! It meant that to me, and believe you me I started from scratch!

Truth is no respecter of persons, only of receptive minds. You may be a walking encyclopedia — a powerful intellect well trained and an orator of first water, but if you have not Truth, you will have to lay down what you have in the end of this, *your conscious world,* that is unlike Truth.

Looking is not the same as seeing —
Nor listening the same as hearing,
But the portal through which all must pass,
If 'tis Wisdom they would grasp.

          F.S.M.

SYMBOLS OF THE AGES

  The circle has always symbolized the All-inclusive Divine Principle or Mind which is static in nature until It moves to create; then, the initial movement is represented by a dimensionless point exactly in the center of this All-inclusive circle of Aliveness.

  The dimensionless point signals the *inception* of an extension of Divine Principle into creative activity. This extension becomes the avenue through which *all* things come into *being*. It is the dynamic Creative Word, Mind, or the "I Am", or the Son or Christ of God. When Principle moves to create, it does so through this extension of itself.

  The first expression of Mind is occupied with creating the *principles* or *rules* of Creation. Next comes the *Substance* out of which springs the invisible beginnings of manifestation in the form of vibratory particles of Light. This Light is but the extension of Mind into its creation. It is the Light that "lighteth every man that cometh into the world." It is the Light that not only looks out of your eyes and mine, but the composition of every atom of so-called matter. It is Divine Intelligence.

  The triangle with its three points, which is often inscribed in the circle, represents three departments in the creative process. Generally speaking, they are first, Divine Mind; second, the creative Word; and third, the reflection or manifest or effect phase. There is a polarity existing between these phases or principles. The circuit maker and breaker is the point called the "Word". It stands in the same relation as the switch that turns on and off the electric activity of the battery in our automobiles. The whole is of the essence of the Godhead — pure Light. This analysis coincides exactly with the Principles of Christianity, rightly understood.

Another symbol of the Ages indicating that Truth and Life are One is the Pyramid Cheops of Egypt. This great architectural pile represents another significant testimony of the laws underlying the creative process. It is called "the Bible in Stone", and it is considered prophetic in that it supports observable universal laws in its construction, history and prophecy. The Pyramid's four sides are perfect triangles, representing the four basic races of mankind, namely: White - Red - Yellow - Black. The converging sides range upward to an apex or tip of the top capstone which, in itself would be if it were there, a perfect pyramid. However, history records it as never having been in place — lending to the idea that the pyramid as a whole is a symbol of the creature called man and the Oneness of all the races — "the Brotherhood of Man". Since some are children in understanding, the spiritual significance of Jesus' statement stands out: "Inasmuch as ye have done it unto the least of these, ye have done it unto Me." Jesus, of course, was speaking as the Christ of God.

The same intelligence that initiated Spiritual Substance, out of which all things are made and composed, framed the universe, built the elements and called them finished — then, filled it with expressions of its life and then, finishing this phase of its work, caused a highly organized animal organism attuned to the requirements of a residence, capable of rendering service as needed by the soul of man to be housed therein. The next phase witnesses the breath of Life itself taking over and thereafter monitoring the human soul in the *extension of the Divine Plan*. This coincides with intuitively guided Adam before his so-called fall, as the Bible story of the Garden of Eden describes it. From this period on, the *effects* inaugurated at this point in evolution began to multiply. Man, an instrumentality of Divine Mind, has filled the earth with wonders on a mounting scale. The same monitoring Intelligence that devised the "Zodiac" that charted the course and the position of each of its signs; that built the Pyramids; that wrote the Bible; that designed the wheel; that built the steam engine; that revealed aerodynamics, clearing the way for the conquest of the air; and to make a long story short, now we are negotiating space, itself. Why should we ask who built the Pyramids? But let us delve a little deeper into the details of this ancient wonder.

Another significant fact concerning the major pyramid of the Egyptian desert is: Long before the modern discovery or revelation of the pyramid's mysteries and architecture, the designer of the back of the great Seal of the United States pictured the top capstone as a spiritual concept of a perfect pyramid in itself. This fact gives a significant key to the symbolic meaning of the pyramid as a whole; namely, it describes the end purpose of the human race and that it is eventually to reach a state of perfection through evolutionary development. Also, it leaves no place or excuse for any department of society to block *progress*. The low passage located at the very entrance of the King's chamber points up civilization's position in true understanding of Reality in the transition from the Aquarian Age to the Pisces Age.

The pyramid's structure, like every material structure, rises from a plan which, in turn, found its inception in the mind of man as a light or an idea. Since one must be alive to think and Life is One, the mind of man is one with the consciousness of the Source of All ideas. It follows, the idea behind the pyramid is an idea in the Mind of God.

The plan upon which the pyramid was built looks like this:

THE PYRAMID'S PLAN AS THE ARCHITECT
SEES IT IN HIS MIND'S EYE FROM ABOVE

Each square represents two steps instead of one of the progressive twelve faculties of man.

A square within a circle, with lines drawn from opposite corners that bisect exactly at the dimensionless point at the exact center of the circle. These lines, together with the sides of the square, form four triangles. The symbolical meaning of the triangle is the Trinity of the Creative Principle. This Creative Principle is all-inclusive, as indicated by the circle. Therefore, the principle includes the four general classified races of mankind progressing toward the perfect spiritual concept of an image of God, symbolized by a small square at the center of the plan. The polygonal base of the pyramid rises from the earth plane, which represents every ingredient or element nature is composed of. These elements were finished before man appeared, as also mentioned above. The pyramid's foundation and interior extends into the earth in such a manner as to show clearly how the physical organism of man is an evolutionary development from the lower forms of animal life. Also, that the ingredients making up the complicated structure of physical man represents every element in nature. If mankind were meant to stay in the animal category and under the animal law of "survival of the fittest" or competition, the indicative tiers of stone rising one above the other and culminating in a perfect spiritual concept of man in the manner which it does, this monumental symbol of the ages no doubt would so indicate. Not to mention the fact that man would not likely be equipped with faculties of understanding if he were not to use them.

Instead, it shows diminishing animal restrictions in the face of spiritual progress from precedents indicative of the Cooperative Principle. Which of course, means to "jointly work together for the same end." I said at the outset, society needs a jolt, so I am warning you now.

Assuming the reader is acquainted with the Archeologist's report on the construction of the Pyramid Cheops and the *writer* has made the *Author's* message clear up to this point, namely, that science and technology working in physics have not only out-distanced orthodoxy's moral and spiritual guidance but, orthodoxy itself violates the principle of evolutionary progress in its own peculiar department of life. Otherwise, *moral* supervision of the inventiveness of science would have long ago prevented its headlong plunge into the all-out manufacture of implements of self-destruction.

Every school of religious belief down through the ages has had its own particular interpretation of Reality expressed in symbols.

The Pyramid Cheops because of its near, if not identical, representation of the Christian concept as expounded by Jesus is herein above briefly explained. There are many others.

Among the foremost in their approach to true Reality are the Chinese schools of Yoga with their elemental discipline of posture designed to bring physical and mental faculties into a relaxed condition of receptivity necessary in any approach to spiritual understanding.

Gautama Buddha achieved perhaps the highest proficiency and therefore still exerts great influence on Eastern religious movements — especially along metaphysical interpretations. The Eastern branch had its origin in the pre-Vedic cults of Trans-Himalaya, whereas the Western branch had its beginnings in Egypt and Chaldea. The Western branch developing along objective lines had perhaps its greatest exponent in Plato and most Greek philosophers.

The Occidental believes what he sees. The metaphysical presentation of invisible forces which must be discerned is of the East. Its acceptance is not easy for the Westerner because of his physical attachments strongly influenced by industrialism. The Hindu places Reality in the invisible and the visible as illusion. The Oriental mind perceives clearly the hierarchies of celestial power.*

Somewhere among the ideologies of the past and present is the Truth of Reality. Hidden from the blind but revealed to the earnest seeker, the naked Truth is revealed in this book. As I have said before, this is the age of ractial adulthood which, by the way, has nothing to do with time and place but with the Realm of Cause — Spiritual Understanding.

Oncoming generations, since time immemorial, have looked to their progenitors for guidance. The orthodox church stands in this position. If it has failed to progress, then it must bear responsibility for the condition of its progeny — a rising tide of problems in an age where mankind is principally engaged in toying with forces beyond the ken of its slide rules and test tubes.

The symbols of the ages have been real guide posts, for they represent true Principle. The ignoring or misunderstanding of them has resulted in countless "isms" and dogmas, all vying for a place in patronage. Unprovable theories may have their rise and fall, but Truth goes quietly and serenely on. The centuries have made not one tiny dent in

* Manly Hall: "Self-Unfoldment".

Its armor. The Master, Jesus, truly outpictured the Truth. But He, too, like the symbols, has been misunderstood and misinterpreted.

More than anything else, it is moral issues that face the world today. It is not a sign of health to neglect morals and at the same time proudly proclaim the giant strides of physical science. To continue this off-balance means anihilation of the human race — not by caprice but by the Divine Law of Cause and Effect. Everyone knows the hour is late — but comparatively few, in or out of the creeds and dogmas, know what to do about it. *True Metaphysics* does not teach us to bury our heads in the sand like the ostrich, but to look at outer conditions with understanding, and *constructively*, rather than destructively, practice through the same principle that through ignorance produced the error.

The answer is clear, once one knows what the trouble is. It is true that we hear from one end of the globe to the other, that education is the answer. *But moral education of the* TRUE *variety is a stumbling block to orthodoxy* — as it was in Jesus' time! More scientists to build better weapons; more students to learn how to make more gadgets for an already complicated economy; more ways to channel unthinking minds into traps that fill the coffers of not only endless services, but dis-services as well; bigger and better churches and cathedrals of the material variety — the better the business organization, the better and fancier the church, no matter what the cost — of course, always *in the name* of our common God, but always at the bottom it is mixed up in some way with *competitive self-interest* and *commercialism*. Always in the pursuit of "Caesar's" dollar and the things it can buy, none of which include the *real* value of a spiritually moral-character. The coin of the material realm is vanity's stock in trade. It isn't the principle, "In God we trust," inscribed upon the dollar that gets the allegiance!

Before Cecil B. DeMille's spectacular picture "The Ten Commandments" loses its interest to the millions who have and who will go to see it, a shocking disillusionment will have set in to hundreds of thousands of those very same people who viewed it.

The reacting thoughts of the reader, if he or she has seen this picture, will determine how much of a shock the shedding of new Light on life will be.

Was it the stupendous strides in the mechanics — the color — properties and the background — the scientific accomplishment in conveying illusionary effects — the masses that were used in portraying the people of that day — the adherence to facts in accordance with history — the debauchery of the fickle followers of Moses — the succumbing of the Israelites to the lure of gold and material wealth they had so long been deprived of; or did the unfolding of this product of scientific advancement give more assurance and understanding and a corresponding lessening of fear of that which is yet to come? Is God still an enigma? Is the rolling back of the Red Sea — the Pillar of Fire — Tablets of the Ten Commandments — the Voice in the Burning Bush factual, or symbols of the spiritual and unchangeable Laws of God? And if the latter be true — where does the cause lie in reference to the terrible things the Egyptian slaves endured in the days of the pharaohs? If Principle decrees that *"a man is as he thinks,"* which is far, far more significant than a mere figure of speech, are not you, the reader, willing to listen to the voice of reason trying to get your attention. A voice, not from the pages of this book, but from the center of your consciousness! The book is but a fulcrum, a stimulator for reasoning thought.

It is difficult for the average person to accept the idea that nothing is hidden from our Divine Father. Our conscience knows how much of a reward or penalty is due us individually. The question is — how deep is conscience buried? Divine Justice never takes time out. We may attend our beautiful churches religiously and people will say how devout we are — because, they too, are judging from appearances. Deep in our hearts we feel guilty *if we are guilty*. If we have cast our lot with Principle and backed up faith with works — *we know it*, and we will receive our earned reward in a measure beyond our fondest hopes. If we are in the path of catastrophe an idea will warn us in time to save us — *if we have done our part*. That is the way Principle protects loyalty. How many times have you, the reader, called Divine Law "Luck"?

It is true our thoughts will out-picture in exact ratio to our thought-pattern. The wretched slavery of the Israelites in Egyptian bondage, in the story, reflected their thought-patterns. This truism is supported, as I have said before, by the time-worn Scripture: "As a man thinketh in his heart, so is he," and his world will reflect back to him what he is in his heart. But what he thinks in his heart are his deep convictions and it is here where conscience (or Divine Justice) will dictate, in accordance with the merits of the case. Religious church attendance or running to a Father confessor is not enough. Lip service is skin deep — "Faith without works is dead." The same principle holds for saint or sinner — it applies equally in attracting the figments of wealth or the eternal treasures we lay up in the heavens of our garden of thoughts. A hackneyed phrase has it that "A man must pay for everything he gets in this world," and I think we should add, also, "in that which is to come."

Jockeying for position to win a war can never win the peace for long. And when the next one comes, as it surely will unless man awakens and very soon, the cost will be multipled — not because of prophesy, I might voice, but because of the immovable Principle of Cause and Effect. The philosophy of Metaphysics deals with "Causes," while Science, the technology of Physics, deals with effects. The same principles that reward us with blessings, penalizes us with disaster, measure for *increased* measure. The cause that appears to be behind our effects, is never *First* Cause. Our deep convictions father every effect, individually and collectively.

"Ye believe in God, believe ye also in the laws and the justice of His domain" — but believe or not, they inhere every moment of our existence! If we really believe in a Divine and Just Law, we cannot, at the same time, look for the cause outside our own selves! In this truism alone lies the answer to the woes of the world!

THE SPIRIT OF THE LETTER

In summing up what has gone before, this fifth chapter rationalizes, for the receptive reader, the seven steps humanity takes, from its first emergence as a self-conscious soul entity until it rises out of the animal realm of nature and assumes the stature of its real purpose: namely, to extend the Father's creativeness in His Divine Plan. The evolutionary development of a *soul* to meet the requirements of Divine Principle takes not merely a life time, but many life times.

The cyclic period of adulthood coincides with the Aquarian Age in which advanced souls will be at home or qualified rulers in their own right — in their own kingdom, under the guidance of the Godhead. Evolution is an Eternal Law of progression. It is the manner in which the poor in understanding advances to knowledge of Truth or Reality. Neither you or I nor the Divine Principle itself alters this law: if it were at all possible there could not be order, much less a standard, which is unthinkable. A Principle without sanctity is "double talk." We can do a lot of resisting only to find ourselves learning the hard way — only finally to realize with chagrin, *when we are ready*, what fools we have been.

Let not the clergy or their adherents or the so-called "man of the street" condemn these truisms without trial under the justice of Divine Law and not the letter of it, which belongs to a passing age.

As I write, the pulpits of many orthodox churches are being invaded by the great saving forces of Metaphysical Understanding. Ministers everywhere are coming to realize the discrepancy between the letter of their Bibles and the Spirit of it. They are beginning to generate the courage of their dawning convictions that they cannot reconcile contradictions found in the letter with the unchanging nature of Divine Principle.

The Septennial Law is the law of 7's, which coincides with the symbolical seven days of creation described in the Scripture. The seasons of the year are not questioned by mankind because they are factually observed. However, the procession of the cycles of 35000-year occurrences of the Cosmos are mathematically arrived at, which reckoning reaches back untold ages beyond our history books. An astronomer mathematically determines the location of a star he cannot see. When a telescope is invented he can see and prove the law of numbers.

As symbolized in the Bible, the seventh day of the time and space week is a day set apart as a day of rest. In reality nature never rests — it only appears to rest while assimilating that which it requires for its growth during its activity. The same principle which is observed in the "microism" holds likewise in the "macroism" of the Creative Process. As represented by the Symbol of the Creative Process (page 183).

The *inception* of a planet into the Creative Process, undergoes a nebulous or gaseous phase before it manifests objectively into the progressive mineral phase. Following the mineral age comes the vegetable, thence the animal and finally the human phase, that is, if a planet has progressed that far. Evidently, the planet Earth has, or man would not be here. The animal-human and its dominating competitive law merges into the surmounting self-conscious Human Race, which has been evolving out from under the dominating animal law from the *beginning* of an awareness in the first species of man. Back of this beginning was the *inception* of the *Idea Man* in the Mind of God. (Your Bible speaks of man being *created* before he ever trod this earth.)

The transition from the Aquarian Age to the Pisces Age is a difficult period for mankind because of his thought habits. His understanding of the abstract side of nature is dim, or as the Bible puts it, "He sees into the mirror of life darkly," or in plain English — life's reflections are not clearly distinguished. These thought habits are binding and difficult to break. I quote, *in spirit,* a biblical reference: "Whatsoever ye shall bind in earth, so ye bind also in heaven," or the heavens of our minds or pattern of our thought processes.

Is it so different today? — It has always taken the shock of violence and suffering on a large scale to introduce new and revolutionary changes in the way society had been in the habit of thinking and living. It is taking place at this moment in many places in the world today.

The eternal skirmishes between Principle and Expedience has now come to an all-out war in the individual — the battle is on. It is a contest between the higher Principle of *Cooperation* and the lower Principle of *Competition.* The battle invades every nook and cranny of society, without exception. Yes, even the edifices of the religious and moral forces, where Christian principles are taught, practice competition in their particular interpretations of Truth. Yet Truth is *Reality* and Reality is Principle and Principle is not influenced one way or the other by opinion or theory

— "God never casts a shadow of turning," and He is One with all Principles — if they are *really* Principles.

Jesus was asked: "What is Truth?" And He stood dumb because He knew His inquirers would not understand because they were not ready. Millions are not ready today and so it will always be — because evolution is an eternal process. But for many of those that *are* ready, it will take violence as well as moral instruction to break the hold of the competitive principle. Only the blind cannot see the mounting contest around the world today — "Man's extremity, God's opportunity," seems to be necessary in this Age. It will take much, much more than the shifting of one error for another to change the picture. The roots of the trouble are not "out there." Science and technology are not so far in advance of spiritual understanding because they have the answers to the mystery of the Ages — but because they have been moving along progressively in their development while the churches have stagnated on old worn-out superstitions of passed Ages. They have established fixities in minds that are, in nature, meant to freely progress.

Fear has driven many people anew to orthodoxy simply because it is an easy way out of the responsibility for thinking these abstract questions out for themselves. The teacher has his definite place — his talents are evidence of this fact. However, his responsibility is manifold that of his listeners. The teaching of true Principles or Divine Law *is* a far-reaching responsibility.

Reality is far and above the theory of any one of the churches regardless of how attractive and grandiose its trappings. In the face of the intrinsic magnitude of the Divine Creator and His Cosmos of Universes the importance of ecclesiastic dogma of the "letter" falls to the level of mere theory. If you ask my authority, an extremely fair question, I assure you — my answer is: A theory that cannot be proved is not worthy of God nor the soul of the man

He created in His image and likeness. Look into your mirror — does it reflect anything but what is put before it? If you can truly answer, "No," and I replied, "You were wrong," you, no doubt, would infer I was impractical and visionary. But there *is* something reflected in that mirror that you didn't put before it. The life that looks out of the reflection of your eyes is intangible, abstract or immaterial. You cannot feel it or touch it but you will not deny it is truly "reflected life" which you are not responsible for being there. Furthermore, if it were not reflected *there*, *nothing could be* reflected there.

To review partly what I have stated elsewhere and to anticipate a question that may be in the reader's mind, "Just what are the qualities of the Godhead?" In the very first place we must realize God, if anything, is All Intelligence, All Power, All Life, All Love, All Spirit, All Light and All Substance, to say the very least. Therefore, He must be Spirit as well as material.

This implies, He is the Essence of all that exists. Also, this implies unlimited freedom of choice. But of the highest importance to the soul of man, created in His image and likeness, is, he too, must also have unlimited freedom of choice when he discovers and proves it for himself. Otherwise, the whole Principle breaks down — or the reflection in the mirror is error.

For brevity's sake I shall use the term, "Mind," since Mind is the Source of all ideas and if an idea in the finite mind of man is a light in the Mind of God it is doubly clear why the Bible depicts Deity as the "Father of Lights." Mind has three aspects. In its unproductive state it is static. In its productive state it is dynamic. In its dynamic state it is the Christ or Creative Principle. Mind's third phase, the manifest phase, is but reflected or transmuted, solidified or objectified Light — limited only by the understanding of the finite mind through which it operates.

From the inception of an idea in the mind of man until we behold its reflection in manifestation, it is but light in essence and that essence is God. "Be still and know that I am God," is a statement of Truth.

These abstract ideas based upon Divine Law will become common usage in this new Aquarian Age which we have already entered.

Now let us speak in terms of the Pisces Age — the Age where the five physical senses have, and are still in the ascendency but, be assured, they will soon be the product of a bygone era insofar as the enlightened soul's position on the "path." It is the *belief* in the *limitations* of the Pisces-Age *material-man*, that is capable of being crucified — not the understanding soul.

A simile is the Principle of mathematics: It also, explains the relationship Mankind holds to the Creative Principle. The digit "1" outpictures the Principle of Mathematics. Until the Principle is put to use by the conscious mind or will, for any purpose whatsoever, it is perfectly static. However, there is no limit placed upon the extent or purpose for which it can be used, except by the individual's "borrowed intelligence" using its inherent perogative of freedom of choice. If there were a limit placed upon its use it could not be a principle. Therefore, it *must* hold true of the reflected Creative Principle inherent in the image of the God-man.

In the face of these foregoing truths, what becomes of the ancient belief that God had to sacrifice the dynamic phase of His own Being, namely, "The Christ of God," in order that mankind be saved from the lessons he must learn for himself before he can raise *his human* out of the animal phase to a comparable level of the Divine Pattern?

Jesus was called the "Way-Shower" and He did show

how the transition of the human soul is accomplished by the renewing of the mind.

Because it is important to remember, I repeat, the soul is cast in eternity and it lives in eternity, now. It is a Spirit entity. The sacrifice of a soul-segment of Spirit (God) is impossible, for Spirit was never born nor can it ever die. It simply "shuffles off this mortal coil" for a better habitation.

The body is of the elements and back to the elements it returns. However, the elements themselves are of the same Essence — pure Light in degree, for another purpose. The story of Golgotha symbolizes the way the human soul must overcome the belief in materiality as being Reality or Principle.

Fear stems from lack of knowledge. Many times we awake from dreams with a sense of great relief. What we commonly call life is often a "nightmare" — and tragically, for it need not be. Only erroneous convictions or misinterpretations of the Master's living message is responsible for the misery and unrest in the world today. And paradoxically, there is as much of this in the church as out of it. If the reason escapes you — you have not received this message! A new-found knowledge awaits the receptive mind that will free him from fear because it acquaints him with Reality. He comes to see the world of effects for what they really are; the solidification of ideas in their entirety; some are in harmony with Divine Purpose and some are not. Nevertheless, all are like the proverbial "bread cast upon the waters," (Ideas cast upon the waters of Thought) — they will return in so many days *multiplied*.

The teaching that truly holds salvation for mankind is called "Metaphysics" because it unifies Spirit, mind and matter into a comprehensive whole that automatically sets at rest fear which is generated by the "unknown." Metaphysics is an unprejudiced study that explains man's place in the scheme of things as well as the relationship he bears to the whole.

The Master was a perfect example of metaphysical understanding. Superstition was no part of His life or teaching. This sort of thing He condemned in the organized church of that day in no uncertain terms. The church He built "was not made with hands." But, many of the hands that built the church of brick and mortar were implicated in His crucifixion.

The plan of life includes man's conversion from the half animal and half human path he is traveling to a spiritually cooperative path in which the higher cooperative Principle is the Law in control. Lincoln voiced a great Principle when he said: "Man cannot exist part slave and part free." Those were comparatively wise words in this age and he, of course, was speaking of the slavery of the South, but the principle applies equally in respect to the real freedom of the individual from the slavery of superstition and sense impressions.

A ship without a rudder is at the mercy of every wind that blows or like a man on a vehicle with a horse hitched to both ends — the strongest physically of the two horses will outpull the other, until he too will be exhausted, with the result that man or beast gets nowhere fast.

In the preface of this treatise, I related an actual experience. This experience illustrates the way one is protected from harm by way of ideas that come into the mind at the opportune time, when one learns to be guided from within. Adam was protected until the evidence of his senses took over. It also illustrates how a continuing allegiance to higher Principle is an insurance against the devastating ups and downs that wear out the material-minded man. This explains the modus operandi of the principle and the promise underlying the 23rd Psalm, when we learn to be guided from within. In my particular case I was in need of a shock of realization — the realization that I was saved from catastrophy for a purpose. *Ideas* in support of this realization came thick and fast into my mind. The "human argument" seemed always to win out over spiritual urges — that is, that I wasn't qualified *yet* to give to the world what I had to give. This attitude, in itself, is a form of fear. Somewhere along the path of every soul's unfoldment it will be beset with fear. In truth, this is the contest that takes place in the conquest of the seeming reality of the outer world of effects and the inner world of Cause. In the case at point, there was no escaping the thunderous voice from within!

An ostrich may bury its head in the sand when a sandstorm is raging. This act, no doubt, provides a sense of security for it allays fear. He does not *see* the storm swirling around his body, and except perhaps for a few missing feathers, he survives the storm and goes about his life as usual. Why does one instinctively turn away from the doctor's needle? How is it that one can wince and actually shut out the feel of a penetrating needle? Why does a doctor engage his patient in conversation when he is about to give a shot, providing he thinks his patient is sensitive to pain? Everyone knows enough about the working of mind to know that an idea of fear cannot be contained at the same instant courage occupies the mind. Also, that the continuous **harbouring of** any idea will, through habit, become automatic. The practice may be constructive or destructive.

Therefore, to focus this analysis down to the process of developing the sixth sense or "intuitive listening in" for guidance — the same procedure is applicable. Using the Master, Jesus, as an example, the souls of men not only have free access to the powers of the Divine, but they were created to use those powers to extend and multiply the inherent creativeness of the Divine Creator.

This spells *progress* in every department of life. The lack of progress at any point of the whole can throw the whole out of balance and eventually pull the whole down to disaster when the case is extreme. Even stubborn resistence to change brings on an extremity and provides an opportunity for God! The Bible and history records the penalty involved in such a condition in its countless descriptions of fallen empires, cities, peoples, families and individuals. And what do we see today by way of stagnation in the most important segments of society? Namely, the lack of attention to the stabilizing moral character in human kind. Man has been given physical senses to *use* with *understanding* — not to deny the factual evidence they perceive. Factual evidence coming to us as ideas do not lead us astray when they are met with *metaphysical understanding*. Whereas, being taken in by appearances is another matter entirely. "Without vision the people perish," is inscribed above the door of a house of learning.

Whatever religious faith one has accepted, the principle of answered prayer never varies. We may beg for something and as long as we are convinced we do not have it, as the begging implies, our prayers are futile. But the moment we get the *idea* or *feeling* our prayers are answered they *are* answered, *by way of ideas*. Understanding and respecting Divine Laws enables one to have the positive feeling. The mysterious *appearance* of some object or condition may seem to side-step the Law of Cause and Effect. However, this one question should automatically provide the answer to the seeming paradox: Can anyone behold, *for himself*, any condition or object without a corresponding *idea* in his mind? I think the reader can answer that question for himself, for, after all, it is simply another way of stating the principle underlying the biblical quotation: "As a man thinketh in his heart, so is he," — and so must his world reflect. Jesus said: (speaking as a human being)

"Unless I go, the Holy Spirit cannot come to you." He was voicing a principle: Unless men and women cease to look or depend on personalities and churches and symbols or superstitional beliefs which, in the last analysis, are "brazen idols," they will find it difficult or impossible to find the Christ within them. When we drink of that Eternal Spring, which Jesus told the woman at the well, sprang up within him, and if him, her as well, she would never thirst — He was voicing a principle applicable to all mankind. (Remember, water means thought.)

The average man or woman attends the "big show" — the "popular personalities" — the "big noise" — or "material wealth" — not the quiet and humble, by popular standards. Yet, it can be said that there are comparatively few who have no regard at all for God in their professed belief. The Master taught love, by practicing it; Divine council by seeking it, in the only place He knew it existed — in the silence of his own heart — and again, he was a "Way-Shower"! "Know ye not, *ye* are the temple of the *living* God? Does not our Lord and our God reign supreme in His Heaven? Know ye not ye are Gods? The Kingdom of Heaven is within you and *at hand*. Why call ye me Lord, Lord and do not the things I say?" The Bible speaks of hypocrits — aren't we all, in more or less degree, until we have made the "exodus" — the march from the lower human-animal phase (Egypt) 'till we reach the level of metaphysical understanding (Promised Land)? Even Peter, called "the rock," upon which Jesus said He built his church, failed Him momentarily. These are patterns of the way man learns. He stumbles until he makes the stumbling blocks "stepping stones" — *always* having freedom of choice. "We pray in secret and are rewarded openly."

We may pray with an idea in mind but, the seed idea will never take root unless watered with faith (or expectant thoughts). "Faith" is the climate of one's thought-pattern.

Without it *nothing* good or evil can happen, for even to *think* implies faith in some degree, negative or positive.

Note the following carefully if you would have *desirable* prayers answered. All manifestation begins with an idea in the imagination. If you really have "faith as a grain of mustard seed" and knowledge to support it, you will know the vision of your desire (the picture in your mind's eye) is already in the creative process and will, by the unseen chemistry of nature (metaphysically called the Subconscious") become a living, breathing fact before your eyes. The only requirement is, to sustain the desired idea with faith and conviction, plus action in the direction of our desires. As long as we *want* for something we have not completed the circuit of the Creative Process — for again, wanting implies *not* having. "When ye pray for a thing, believe ye receive it and ye shall have it." When we understand the way the mind works, through the lens of Metaphysics, our knowledge keeps pace with faith. So here again should be convincing evidence that there is no quarrel with denominational religion, only with erroneous and unprovable interpretations of Divine Principle. How can one be sure? I answer, one can prove that some fixities of ecclesiastic dogma are diametrically opposed to freedom and progress which are basic principles which is the nature of God.

Any change in the outer world of an individual is in exact correspondence to the pattern of that individual's convictions. No man, priest or God can be responsible for the work of learning the lessons each living soul must do for himself. He can only point the way. A man's "yoke" becomes easy, when and as he permits himself to be guided from the *seat of conscience* within.

The story of the Garden of Eden gives us a metaphysical pattern of how man is meant to live in accordance with Divine Law. Also that he receives Divine guidance by way of his conscience at the center of his consciousness, ("in the midst of the garden"), as distinguished from any physical location in the body.

Conscience Itself is the dynamic life principle. It is the "God of the living — not of the dead." According to Scripture a person may be "*dead* in his trespasses and sins" yet, apparently living. Also, that a person really lives only in the consciousness of Truth.

The Source of Divine Thought is the Spring in the midst of the Garden that wells up, giving man a sense of eternal livingness. As long as Adam remained constant to this Source he had access to all the Garden had to offer.

The moment he began to look to outer effects — depending upon his reactions to outer effects — or trusting to sense judgment (the Serpent), he began to "eat of the tree of the *knowledge* of good *and* evil." In other words, he began to ascribe power (in his convictions) to that which has no power — he began to deny God his Creator and Sustainer — to look to effects for cause.

The Bible says: "Have no other Gods besides Me." Also, the Garden of Eden story tells us that God warned Adam that if he did eat of the tree of the knowledge of good and evil he would surely die. Not only die, but until he did, he would have to earn his bread by the sweat of his brow.

Symbolically, the "brow" locates the seat of the will. If one depends upon a will severed from God he will truly sweat in the task of solving his problems. He will find himself limited and helpless before the competitive storms of the material world.

To be in league and partnership with our Creator is to lose fear of death. So much for the Garden of Eden story.

Now as to Freedom — *Real freedom* does not exist *outside* of Divine Law. Material bars of steel and stone cannot hold a *spiritually free* man, no more than material wealth can make a man rich, no more than a castle can make a real home, for the very simple reason that *ideas* are qualities, whether love, happiness, health, material wealth, or success in any category — or the very negative opposite. *Without* ideas one is poor indeed! And none, if they think at all, are really poor. As the theme of a popular metaphysical song goes: We can "build a cathedral deep down in our hearts" or we can build a veritable hell and in either case we do it with the self-same power, "in the Father's name, I." When you are ill — or when you feel well, or when you are happy, do you not proclaim the fact in the First Person, or "I?"

"One ship drives east, and another west,
   With the self same winds that blow,
'This the set of the sails, and not the gales
   Which tells us the way they go.

"Like the waves of the sea are the ways of fate,
   As we voyage along through life,
'Tis the set of the soul which decides its goal,
   And not the calm or the strife."
                      — *Ella Wheeler Wilcox*

It is hoped the moral forces of human society will not ignore the import of this eleventh-hour appeal for understanding-solidarity. To do so means missing, perhaps, the greatest opportunity ever to come their way. Or turning their backs on the salvation of the race in this Age. Or the unity resulting from understanding. Said Jesus: "I would have mothered them as a hen her chicks but they would not." "*They*" crucified Him instead— why? Because "*they*" were mentally shackled to erroneous beliefs!

This message is not for a "stickler for the letter" — He will fly to the Bible and crucify on the strength of the "letter". After all, it was the convictions of the adherents of the letter of the church's text-book of that day, 1900 years ago, that was responsible for the crucifixion of Jesus. They would not accept the Spirit of the letter which Jesus came to teach. Again, why? And again I answer: Because of non-progressive fixities of belief — stagnation, the forerunner of material death.

Let us read again that wonderful reflection:

"It is *never error* for a person or a people or a nation to learn distasteful things about itself; rather, a privilege and a Divine blessing in disguise, if in the Spirit accepted."

All of the parables in the Scriptures have their spiritual meaning. To name a few which this authority states, "The letter killeth but the Spirit giveth life," the "Garden of Eden" is the garden of thoughts, emanating from our conscience the seat of the indwelling Christ that is within us all. "When we sit at the feet" of the only Son of God and be guided by His inspirational advice, *we are 'practicing the Presence'*. When we eat of the "Tree of the Knowledge of Good and Evil" (or ignorance of the Truth of Reality) we depart from the Divine Laws of our being. We have been listening to the serpent in the jungle of material thinking. When a Buddhist monk burns himself to death before passersby in the middle of a city to gain favor in the eyes of a "God of Parts and Passions" — clearly he is shackled to a traditional but erroneous conviction. Our so-called civilized society has just as many negative convictions of a Creator that can be swayed from the immovable Laws of His Being.

As I have stated elsewhere, the return of our Savior in the clouds, which millions are waiting for — which metaphysical interpreted means — A new dispensation of understanding is dawning in the heavens of those of us that are ready for and open-minded enough to receive this rewarding salvation. Again, "When the Disciple is ready, the Master appears."

Just one more translation, God does not set aside the Laws of His Being, which would be the case if He were to sacrifice His only-begotten Son — the Christ of God — the Word of God, or the Lord God, which is none other than the Dynamic Phase of the Father, Himself, that indwells us all. Jesus, the human abode of the Christ, was crucified not to save the world from the Law of Cause and Effect but because of the ignorance of the Truth of Reality in the world then, as it is now. Yes, the Age of Aquarius — the age of new Spiritual Understanding — is upon us now — *and now is the propitious time*. There is no tomorrow for anyone of us, for when tomorrow arrives it will still be today to us. Eternity has no time limitation, nor have the souls of mankind, for they are created in the image of our Divine Creator.

As for myself, the unfinished business of my purpose in the plan of Divine Intelligence is to record what inspirationally comes pouring into my consciousness guided by my conscience. All human beings are not here without a purpose. What their equipment is at this point of their soul's progressive journey depends upon their progenitors in heredity. What our forefathers were in thought and action will reflect in their children unto the third and fourth generations.

Repeated affirmations form habits of thought and action. If they are constructive — we build positive life-outlook stances on 'solid ground' experiences, so to say. The writer is using this method with this fact in mind. Especially because the subject matter may be unfamiliar to many people.

Chapter VI

METAPHYSICS THE AMALGAMATING PRINCIPLE

Metaphysics, the semantics of religion, speaks in terms of the soul of man. It characterizes one of the three points of the Triangle that symbolizes the Trinity, that is, it brings together in understanding the spiritual and physical or material phases of creation. Metaphysics shows basically how the soul reflects that which *the soul conceives itself to be* — or interprets factually, psychologically and materially, that which the individual has come to really believe about life and his relation to it.

Metaphysics explains and therefore saves through the mental gyrations of reason and logic, the *unifying connecting link* between abstract Cause (or God) and the psychological and material effects in nature. It is philosophy plus the *spiritual* meaning that underlies the letter of our Bibles. Whereas philosophy alone means, "the pursuit of knowledge of the causes of all phenomena both of mind and matter." Without an understanding of this principle the soul operates on blind faith — on what appears to be true. Understanding of it puts solid ground not only under the spiritual meaning of the Master's teaching, but the laboratory tests of science. Man can never reach solid rock in his convictions until his convictions are supported by knowledge. Solomon said: "With all thy getting, get understanding." One cannot acquire understanding unaccompanied by knowledge. Though closely allied, the terms are not perfect synonyms. Knowledge implies practice-supported truth, whereas, understanding may still remain in the category of theory.

Metaphysics introduces the "New Age" of Aquarius — the Age of Spiritual adulthood — the Age of moral thought and reason. Aquarius means "water" and the translated meaning of "water" in the Bible is thought — as mass thought is spoken of as the "seas" — as I have mentioned heretofore for emphasis.

Have you ever read the Bible with this in mind? If you haven't, I urge you to do so.

Metaphysics implements the shedding of the Pisces Age, the twelfth sign of the Zodiac, of partial understanding — culminating one's "wandering in the dark" of the *Truth of Reality*. It is the fulfillment of the Truth of Reality which the Master came to teach.

A man may accept factual evidence as truth and the world will reflect back to him that which he has accepted. Only metaphysics can reveal the truth of his assumptions through understanding and knowledge of the Creative Principle.

Metaphysics develops the "sixth sense" which, in its higher phase, is extrasensory in nature. Metaphysics ennables the reasoning faculties to discern the spiritual significance of the *letter* or our Bibles.

THE AUTHENTICITY OF THE ZODIAC

Is it not strangely significant that the "Zodiac's Aquarius" is timely as a signal for the renewing of the mind since it represents the "water carrier" which in translation means idea or thought action. The Master taught this principle.

Also, note that Aquarius is followed by the Pisces Age — representing the "fish" — the Biblical symbol of Jesus, "the fisher of men."

The authenticity of the Zodiac comes down through astronomy and astrology's mathematical study of the various constellations of the heavens sometime before the Hellanistic period — a development in Mesopotamia — which authoritatively turned out to be accurate definitions.

As these thoughts come to me, and the way they come, I accept their inspirational nature as an aspect of the Truth of Reality.

There are many teachers who follow the metaphysical view of Christian principles who are in error when they interpret Solomon's axiom: "As a man thinketh in his heart, so is he" to mean one should see everything in this world in a rosy light without understanding.

To be blind to the ills of the world does not coincide with the Master's purported behavior. For He saw blindness, disease and wrongdoing in the world of His day just as He would today. Obviously, He had to see with his human, physical eyes where error manifested, in order to prescribe a cure in keeping with the Christ Principle in Him (His consciousness).

Discerning everything good in its basic essence does not mean seeing everything good when the wrong combination of thoughts have resulted in an unhealthy condition.

One cannot blame God for the evils of the world — only the ignorant application of His Laws by us human beings.

So, emphasis falls again upon the importance of learning the nature and purpose of Universal Principles. To think creatively is to think with understanding.

In order to understand the unchangeable laws of life correctly from Christendom's point of view, one must take the trouble to thoroughly digest the significance of the more than fifty titles given the Christ of Jesus found in the "Subject Index" of the teacher's copy of the King James version of the Holy Bible. In the same section will be found a long list of Biblical types and symbols of the Christ.

Even a brief consideration of this information plainly indicates Christ is a *Principle* inherent in every human soul. A Principle which truly arrives in consciousness in the manner of an *Immaculate conception.*

Also, by the same token, the human animal organism comes *into being* in exactly the same manner as any other animal organism. Jesus, the human, was no exception. The Divinity attached to Jesus was in His development from a lower to a higher stage of understanding — to a divinely spiritual concept of Reality. The Bible tells us, all have sinned in Adam (i.e., the human).

It follows as day the night all must be spared through meeting the requirements of known Universal standards — standards that are proven over and over every day of our lives.

Unprogressive human interpretations of Divine Laws as promulgated by way of traditional dogmas and creeds are proving in our reflecting times *how in error* they are. The Principle of "Cause and Effect" permits of no ignorance in respect to its nature. Nor does the Principle of *Progress.* Be you peasant or king, or any of the grades between, you cannot escape the power of either one of these principles. There are others of equal importance that will come up for consideration in this book.

Every book counter, every library, and every source of ancient knowledge carries manifold writings that speak of and promise a revelation of the *Secret of the Ages,* hidden from all but the elect. Some will hint the All-Mighty is discriminatory, but for a price God can be circumvented.

Self-help books abound. Talented writers make things simple *if* the aspirant will follow directions.

It is true that much Truth finds its way into the hearts and minds of receptive souls through easy lessons. And frankly, if it were my purpose, I, too, would be imparting my message in like manner.

The true seekers of the wisdom that knowledge of Divine Laws impart will eventually come abreast of the so-called "forbidden secrets of the masters." The formula, if it can be called that, is *desire* supported by a strong will and a teachable receptivity — following the lead of instructors who, in turn, are guided by known Universal Principles — not dogma.

Miracle methods, if they bring results, will always turn out to be but the proper application of Divine Law.

There is one thing the uninitiated should get straight at the outset. All *Universal* Principles are Divine. The wise bases his thought and action on them with understanding. The ignorant also may believe he is doing the same. How can one be sure, you ask. The answer must always be "by the manifest effects" for they will be in direct relation to *"First Cause"*.

As one writer has said in part: Knowledge of the abstract principles of life cannot be bought and sold in the market place — not property that can be traded or pulled off the shelf and transferred to just any mind, until that mind is ready.

On the other hand, when that mind is longing, praying and seeking an understanding of Reality and will pay the price of attention and follow the lead of reason, he will gain the treasure of all treasures which embodies: health where one has been ill; abundance where poverty has dogged one's footsteps; happiness and security where there has been misery and loneliness; and love where there has been hate; charity where there has been selfishness;

confidence where there has been timidity; courage where there has been fear; strength where there has been weakness; purpose where confusion has reigned; a world that smiles one's way because one smiled its way from the heart — not from behind a mask of suspicion and distrust. The advance of personal years adds security and peace of mind, not frustrations. One looks forward into the unknown with assurance because the Principles he or she has come to understand are Eternal, not temporal.

The path leads upward and onward into ever-widening vistas of beauty and harmony.

If I write in unfamiliar terms, I suggest the reader procure any one or more of any of the lists of "self-help" books. I am impressed to mention "The American Idea of Success" by Richard M. Huber.

"Shorthand" adequately tells the story to one familiar with shorthand terms. In the art field of endeavor, "water color" is sometimes called "shorthand painting." All lines of endeavor have their method of briefing a subject. The writer appears to strike a happy medium that seems to fit his nature. My aim is to share a message based upon my eighty-eight years of concentrated effort in the direction of the subject of this book, not the merchandising of the book itself.

If it were my purpose to single out what is more palatable to the *unrealistic* way society is inclined, I would have done so — but the urge is too powerful in the way I have chosen.

As Jesus is purported to have said in substance: "I came not to take away the law but to bear witness to it." Likewise, the unfoldment of the knowledge metaphysics provides, brings to mankind an era of blessed well-being through greater understanding of the laws and not to displace them — to engender greater respect for the Creator and the Sustainer of all that is — not to do away with the God "that was before Jacob" but to *magnify His name!*

Metaphysics explains how, by law, an idea once in the mind of man will germinate and manifest in exact accordance with the degree of a knowingness supported by active faith. "Active faith" implies — faith with works and deeds." Metaphysics proves the Scripture that states: "Ask whatsoever ye will in My Name, believing, and it shall be granted unto you as you believe."

Metaphysics is a study that cannot be explained in a few paragraphs nor is it the purpose of this book to attempt to do so, but rather to bring to the fore those things necessary in any successful solution to the problems the world is faced with today.

"HE THAT IS NOT AGAINST ME IS FOR ME"

Metaphysics explains the significance of the Zodiac as it explains the underlying significance of the teaching of the Master, Jesus. Science has proven that all things have a nucleus or center around which the smallest to the largest atomic manifestation revolves. The Zodiac's twelve signs symbolize the twelve faculties of man as it does the twelve departments of nature or the twelve eras or ages or cycles the earth and its satellites pass through before it repeats itself, ever expanding. Before the soul of man (the real man) has mastered the twelve lessons, through experience, he has not gained the stature of the Christ. Until he does, he must repeat the process until he has. The soul is not fully qualified as an image of the Creator until he can, as the Bible puts it, "sit at the right hand of God." Until then he is not qualified to administer the Kingdom exactly as does the Father.

As has been said elsewhere — "the soul is cast in Eternity," not by caprice but for a definite purpose — and not to haphazardly fail of that purpose. The soul arises by law and its end purpose will be accomplished by law. Its purpose is to extend the creativeness of the Principle that gave rise to it. The physical instrumentalities it functions through are incidental to its needs. What the human being, which is called man, sees with his limited senses can hardly provide a reliable picture of the real man and his relation to the great plan eternally unfolding. As he comes to understand the Creative Process and the wrong use of the hand he has in it and how this fact is responsible for his troubles, he changes his world by changing his attitudes toward it.

Now how do we go about this requirement? As it comes to me — first by assuming an open mind . . . by listening to the still, small voice within. "Except ye become as a little child, ye can in no wise enter the Kingdom of Heaven", so said the Master.

He was not speaking of a place in the skies, but a place in the consciousness of mankind — or the heavens of human understanding. Children are teachable and adults are only grown up children on a pathway of learning. Life-Love-Law-Faith-Progression. Those are the characteristics of the path. We are all on that path or we would not be here today.

I quote again that wonderful observation: "It is never error for a person, a people, or a government to learn distasteful things about itself". This may not be the exact letter of the statement, but I am sure it is the spirit of it, and the personality who said it knows that it is, for he holds the highest position the people can bestow upon a person in these United States.

Chapter VII

THE IMPLICATION OF METAPHYSICS IN POVERTY AND DISTRESS

Many are confused as to the meaning of the terms, "conversion" and "salvation". They are not strictly synonymous terms as used in the biblical sense. One may be converted from one direction of habitual thinking to another and in terms of Christianity, a healing takes place — and it can be instantaneous. If the switch in belief is deep and abiding, the new concepts get good rootage in the subconscious. If the new seed-concept falls on hard, resisting soil, so to speak, it will have difficult, if any, permanency. Therefore, the healing is likewise temporary in degree of the receptivity of the recipient. Transversely, a deep and sustained conviction grows into a deep and abiding faith and the fruits of this union with Truth will multiply with each planting of active faith. "Active faith" implies working at it or giving off of the quality one wishes to acquire. The *simulation* of the qualities of Truth is *salvation*, in the degree it is accomplished. The *acquired* understanding of *Truth is dynamic power* in whatever way it may be used — it also carries with it moral *responsibility*.

The responsibility implies exemplary expression of Divine character. Ideas are God's "coin of the realm"; therefore, the giving off of the wealth of the Divine nature is the giving of real treasure. To the extent the writer is actively carrying out this principle he attracts an abundance of ideas, proving the efficacy of the Law in the category of "Metaphysical Philosophy." Because of its overall importance the writer has made metaphysics his choice. The same Law applies to every department of learning.

The following illustration affords an excellent example: "A" loans $10.00 to "B" without interest, and when "B" returns the $10.00, "A" gives it back to "B" and tells him he is to keep it until someone else comes along who needs it and then he, too, is to loan it to them under the same terms he received it — each would have use of the money *temporarily* without gain. But, if "A" gives "B" an *idea* and tells him to give it to some other person in need of an idea and "B", in turn, tells the recipient of *his* gift to do likewise, all will not only be giving of intangible but, *real wealth,* but he or she will at the same time be *retaining* and *maintaining* a steady flow of the same real wealth. This shows the difference in real and temporal wealth. "To he that *hath* (in mind) shall be given, and to he that hath not, even that which he hath shall be taken away."

A traveler returning from an around the world tour, when asked what impressed him most, replied, "Poverty and starvation." India, especially, has nurtured the idea of scarcity for centuries. Their most revered *teachers* have practiced withdrawal from society. This philosophy is erroneous. It sets up an example that becomes fixities of thought and expression which the teeming millions automatically and religiously follow. It is not difficult for one who knows the principle of giving (Cause) and receiving (effect) to discern the reason for their poverty.

The same law that brings this condition to Asia brings economic abundance to these United States. India has its teachers — United States has its leaders in educational standards. Asia has abundance of the basic elements just as has the U. S. A. The sages of Asia are wise in many departments of metaphysical understanding but they err in withdrawing from human society, for in so doing they are not sharing their ideas and knowledge of Truth with their brothers and sisters.

Advanced Metaphysics recognizes oncoming generations who must learn and therefore earn the ability to overcome the material world. Peace and happiness are not dependent upon *"things"* and the continual wanting of things. "Man does not live on bread alone." The sages have learned this truth and enjoy the knowledge and ability to live it. But they have *their* own peculiar calling. Misinterpretation of the meaning of their exemplary lives by their followers works an acceptance of poverty as the will of their Deity. Poverty, in any category, is a stage on the pathway of a soul's evolutionary unfoldment of understanding. The Western world, despite its accomplishments, has its inhibitions also. Yes, it too, lacks understanding of its Great Exemplifier — the Way-Showing Jesus.

The Master, Jesus, practiced *understanding* of the relationship of all things and how creation comes into existence. He practiced the meaning and scope of metaphysics. Broadly speaking, that is the aim of this treatise.

METAPHYSICS AND THE SOUL'S SURVIVAL

The soul is of the same essence as its Source. Its Source is pure Spirit or pure Light or Substance. It is All-in-All — All consciousness — All ideas, in whatever phase of development an idea may be undergoing. The soul of man, being of the essence of God in whom he lives and has his being, whether on this material plane or not, is never outside the mind of God as an idea, created to carry out "The Plan." The soul's work, in *this particular class-room* of his education, has its beginning and ending. The ending of this life's span is but the beginning of another, yet, the soul stands in the same relation to its Source as it has and always will. As will be observed, all nature has its rest periods, during which it assimilates the lessons or experiences while actively engaged. When Jesus was asked what takes place when one dies to this world, He said in essence: "Thou shalt stand in thy lot until called. The soul of man survives because of his nature and purpose. One door closes, another opens. Always progressively upward in understanding — but not always weighted down with a worn out "mechanism," and never in advance of the soul's level of growth. When that level is sufficiently raised, the soul will no longer need a material body."

An ancient axiom runs something like this: "Any idea that will tend toward establishing in the individual, independence of thought, will gain support of Universal Law." Simply because, man was created to learn his own lesson — to pull his own weight — to make his own bed — to captain his own soul — to reflect his own Godhead — and transversely, any idea that tends to shackle freedom of thought is anti-Principle to the extent the infraction is practiced. — And I repeat again: It is always true that we do so "in the Name of the Father" — or "I." The same principle adheres in the modern metaphysician's axiom — "Any idea that will magnify Principle in the mind of the individual is in league with the Allmighty and, through the law that says, "Like attracts like," will automatically attract to itself that which is its own," — therefore, let me quote again: "To each his own."

The Scripture that states: "The last enemy to be overcome is death," to most minds, is a dim if not utter impossibility. The accepted conviction is: The surest thing in this world is "taxes and death!" And the average person thinks it a waste of time to even consider that it might or might not be true. However, unless my wires got crossed somewhere, "death" to the soul of man, in the meaning of the context, is a scientific and metaphysical lawful impossibility!

Man has not discovered a limit to space. He has, however, found all things revolve around a center, and that planets evolve from a nebulous of cosmic dust. This "dust" of the cosmos constitutes every element in matter, as does the dust of the earth we live on. These *elements*, the Bible tells us, were and are finished products of God. The soul of man is the breath or life of God. Man's material body is the sum of every ingredient in nature or the dust of the elements. However, these elements are themselves but solidified light. This, too, is in agreement with the Bible.

The elements of the planets, that were completed, go on and on continually expanding in limitless space, continually changing in composition and higher complexity in eternal transition. Man's destiny is to likewise go on continually renewing himself — continually multiplying the vehicle that serves as a temple for the Living God. Science and Scripture again support each other in this interpretation.

Bodies that wear out do so first in the conviction of the soul's consciousness. Bodies will continue to die for the simple reason that material creation is a continual process, as stated above, but the *soul* of man is Spirit and is created to become a fully qualified agent, as Jesus became the Christ and no longer needed to return to a material classroom for further instructions. Furthermore, Jesus, in His life in the world of effects, *performed* the necessary works by *being* or living the part of a truly qualified Son of God. He, therefore, raised His human self to a Divine level by *works*.

Again be reminded, Christ Jesus was a "Way-Shower" and not a sacrifice and the Christ in you and me is still the "Way-Shower." Among dozens of Scripture references in support of this Truth we have this: Christ is called the "Word of God" and in John I, we are told, "In the beginning was the Word and the Word was with God and the Word *was* God." It follows, God does not sacrifice that which He is.

When Jesus, the human, had erased all the power of material concepts to influence Him, His creative thoughts merged with the Divine purpose. "Calvary's Cross" symbolizes that passage, not only for Jesus, but all mankind. Jesus died *because* of the sins of the world — not *for* the sins of the world!

Sin is ignorance of *reality!* The "Father of Lights" could not have set aside the Law of His Being in the activating phase of Himself, which, again, is the Christ of God. Christ is both the Son of God and the S-U-N of God. The Bible tells us this, too, when it says: "*I Am* (the light of the world) the Light that lighteth every man that cometh into the world."

Jesus showed in His transition that every soul-entity survives death of the human body. Man was made to live, not to die. Only when he has *learned* and *earned* the knowledge of how to live in accordance with his purpose in Creation will he no longer find it necessary for him to discard worn-out vehicles. This is the same as saying: Man is to live in the *Spirit* of the Christ, the dynamic phase of God Himself. Speaking as the Christ, Jesus said, "I and the Father are One and I in you and you in Me." Or, the outer human is but a reflection of what the soul conceives itself to be. If the soul of man (a spiritual entity) lives in the Spirit of the Christ of God, he really reflects that Spirit both inwardly and outwardly.

If we were to strip the Bible of its historical and factual significance, we would have a perfect Textbook of the Laws of Life.

The Trinity of the Creative Process bespeaks *progress* of human understanding. Lack of understanding, or ignorance, is dying, according to ordinary world concepts.

Man has freedom to prolong the process but not the end-purpose of his existence!

The following axiom may be shocking to some minds but it stands up to the test of Principle: Any idea that establishes the true relationship of Spirit and matter in the mind of the individual is the second coming of the Savior. It is the metaphysical or completing factor of philosophy that completes the circuit of the polarity the Trinity symbolizes: A Principle that always existed, but lost sight of, in the mind of man.

"When ye were children, ye thought as children but now ye are in adulthood and must come to think as adults." This is the spirit of a Scripture which Bible students will recognize. The metaphysical interpretation of the Bible prophecy that tells of the return of the Lord Jesus Christ in the Heavens is: "The return of the knowledge of Truth in the heavens of thought." The prophecy also speaks of the "first fruits" being caught up in the skies of Heaven. The first fruits are those that have become aware of the metaphysical meaning of Life. The "second resurrection" in the same prophecy refers to those who, after difficulty, finally are lead to accept the New Order, and then, they too, will be joyfully reconciled to the heavenly or true way of seeing things.

Principle is not subject to orthodox convictions but orthodoxy is subject to Principle. "Righteous Judgment" is based on Principle or Truth, or Reality. Never on mere opinion — and he who would judge righteously must be established in Principle.

Principle says, there is no right and wrong way; there is only the right way. Scripture warns not to eat of the tree of the *knowledge* of *Good and Evil,* and to do so, one dies — to Truth. At the same time we are told to eat of the tree in the midst of the garden (the center of consciousness, or garden of thoughts or conscience). Thoughts are ideas. A garden has to be watered with good thoughts:

good thoughts emanate from conscience and conscience is Principle — and Principle is God.

How do we come to know this for ourselves? The answer is: Through the great Revelator — the study of the abstract relationship of all things which goes by the name of "Metaphysical-Philosophy" (for the purpose of this treatise) because, metaphysics is a higher phase of philosophy. Jesus, the Master Teacher, was first of all, a metaphysician, for He knew the Law so well that He became One with it in Spirit and in Truth. He did not organize a church and dogmatically teach His philosophy of life. He did, however, select twelve men from different walks of life, each having characteristics of one of the twelve faculties of man. He told these disciples to go and teach the Kingdom of God is at hand.

Jesus was purported to have said, "Know ye not ye are the temple of the *living God?*" which places heaven within our garden of thoughts — and He placed God, the Father of all that is, in His Heaven. We may make what we will of Jesus' teaching, for we do have "freedom of choice" but, if we choose the sword, we will, through the Law of Cause and Effect, die by the sword.

Justice may weep for the condemned but there could be no justice without Law. Jesus wept, too, before Jeruselem and is purported to say: "I would have gathered them as a hen her chicks but they would not."

The writer knows the "Author" is not trying to force the Truth on any reader considering this message; however, he also knows these words will not return to him void. Those who have been running to outer mediators to unload their troubles when the only Mediator there is, is nearer than their very breath — it is they who will feel this message threatens to rob them of their only hope of salvation, but if they only knew, it is the very opposite. To them I say, "Let go and let God" — "Be still and *know* that *I Am God"* and there is none other. Any other mediator is false if he says he can stand up for us — he can only show us how to contact for ourselves, the Christ within.

Please let me remind the reader again, when the outer you says "I", you are speaking in the Father's name — not displacing Him. Our own Bible says: "Ask whatsoever ye will in my name, *believing*, and it shall be granted unto you as you believe." *Being* something in *your* mind and *knowing* it is already in the Creative Process, and keeping faith with this Truth, is tantamount to answered prayer, but our convictions outpicture a negative condition just as sure as it will a positive conviction.

The nebulous stage of the Creative Process is the imaginary phase. We do not see it but we discern it with the faculty of discernment. The only place to alter or cancel out an undesirable manifestation, in the making, or already outpicturing in the factual world of effects, is in that imaginary formative phase where the roots are anchored. This Principle is at work at all times though we may be totally unaware of it. The patient is always our erroneous fixities of mind. An open mind is ready for the Truth. A closed mind is not. "Except ye become as little children, ye can in no wise enter the kingdom of God."

The reader is now receiving a glimpse of the wonderful *Revelator* coming in the clouds of his imagination for which millions are looking to the physical skies above to see a Saviour that greets the eyes — instead of a dawning awareness in the heavens of mind. I repeat what Solomon said: "With all thy getting, get understanding." That is exactly what a dedicated study of metaphysics will do for any one who will put forth the sustained mental effort — who wants to know more than the mental effort required.

Perhaps the reader may ask the writer what *he* expects in the advent of an all-out atomic war, relative to his own personal safety? My answer is: Fifty years' test-proving of the principles espoused herein has formed the fixity of conviction in my outlook that, no matter the tempest that rages around me, I will in some way be protected. No doubt, the outer physical reason will be called accident or coincidence. Just as many other experience the writer has had were called "luck." In the preface I related an experience, one of many I have had, which serves as an example as to how protection comes in natural ways in exact accordance with the Law of Cause and Effect. You remember the story of Job wherein he said, "The thing I so greatly feared has come upon me." The conviction — the idea — the assurance he felt of impending personal trouble worked out in exact relation to the Law of Cause and Effect.

Now just let us suppose that I succumbed in the flesh under the condition existing at the time. How would I view such an occasion? There was a time in my life that I would have worried about such an eventuality and attracted just such a situation. That was before I understood many of the mysteries that metaphysics reveals. Now, I know when my work is finished, a great new adventure opens before me.

Do you ask what I think it will be like? Again I answer: The soul of me is cast in Eternity. What I have learned of eternal Principles and made *my own* — my own will remain with me. Understanding of eternal Principles are the treasures one "lays up in heaven." They have been earned and paid for in "the coin of the realm," that is, Ideas of Truth and Reality. Not the by-product the outer man which "Caesar's realm" holds as constituting wealth. No one can take that kind of wealth with them, for it is but a reflection of the real. It can be relatively positive or negative — still it is but a ghost of the genuine.

No human soul graduates from a lower grade classroom to a higher, except he passes the test. The principle of education in our schools is based upon this law of progression. Why should one expect to escape it on the eternal plane?

What should anyone do to get in step with Divine Purpose? My answer again is: Learn the language of the New Era and as this is done and in the degree of each succeeding light or idea of Truth one comes to understand — "Go and sin no more!" And then, *be assured,* the Master was speaking the Truth when He said: "Neither do I condemn thee, thy sins have been forgiven."

Can one suppose for one minute that those *very religious,* saving peoples around the world (and in our socalled civilized society, which we must admit exists) really had the understanding Solomon voiced way back in Biblical times?

Are we so sure our institutions of higher learning have taught us the real Truth about Reality? That which must stand up to the unimpeachable Divine Standards, which of necessity, if correct, must be *moral* in essence or Principle? Do you realize it is the "intelligencia" (the socalled Establishment) that set the standards of our civilized society — and we must admit the larger portion practice some form of religious beliefs — *"beliefs,"* yes, but I cannot believe it is their *"convictions"* — or our civilization would be headed in the more constructive end purpose God ordained for it.

Mankind will perform as they have been taught. If the teachers are grounded, so to speak, in true standards and teach them accordingly, so will their receptive students follow the impressions they received. On the other hand, the Bible has the word for it — "When the blind lead the blind, *they all fall in the ditch."*

Monks burning themselves to death, not to mention thousands around the world, in lesser or greater degrees, offering up their lives which God has granted them. Can we suppose the Master was in error when He said, "Neither do I condemn thee. Go and sin no more." He was speaking in the Spirit of the Christ of God (the dynamic phase of the Father, Himself) which indwells us all.

Where must the responsibility lie? Hopefully, there are but few who *cannot* answer that.

There was a time when the only thing that was real in my concept of life was what I could cognize with my five physical senses. That was before I learned the meaning of the term "discernment," or "*mental seeing.*" Metaphysics showed me that all things have their roots in the abstract "ideating" area of "First Cause" — or the imagination.

Ignorance of these seemingly A B C's of Reality still afflicts society today or the answer to the riddle of what to do to turn the tide of deterioration would be outpicturing in constructive trends.

These truths are open to all who will listen. They have been imparted to those who have reached a degree of receptive understanding of true spiritual reality through inspirational guidance. All have these occult, sixth sense qualities. The uninitiated will question this statement for many believe this quality is reserved only for special people outside the universal laws of God, just as many brilliant minds educated in accredited institutions of higher learning cannot accept one on equal terms who has not had these advantages.

For those who have accepted the Master's teaching should remember that Jesus did not discriminate in His selection of His disciples — not to mention that the writer was a 'drop-out' from the fourth grade. Even my beloved wife has spoken of me as 'unbelievable'. I have lived these eighty-eight years — a step-by-step progressive pathway — because I am blessed with a thirst for 'understanding' — Solomon's kind.

Chapter VIII

BY WHAT AUTHORITY?

"By What Authority" is a question often asked but seldom adequately answered. We have been rationalizing the reliability of Universal Principles. Just how much can one digress from them and still come up with the right answers? My answer is none whatever — if we want mathematically correct answers.

We all know that Science long ago began to learn the reality of physical laws that adhere in what is called "Mother Nature." The slightest disregard for these principles sometimes proves disasterous. In the higher echelon of this phenomena of Universal Laws the rule of exactitude is no less apparent to a critical observer.

Perhaps the telling of what I saw some time ago on television will illustrate: On a popular program I watched a marvelous demonstration of how the slightest error, due to ignorance of the laws of "Electro-Dynamics," can be disastrous.

There was a tall oblong-shaped device about twelve or fifteen inches square and about six feet high. About eight feet away stood another such device; this one was only about four feet high. The guest with a secret wrote his name on a blackbord and whispered his secret to the MC. The audience saw the secret spelled out on their T.V. screens but the panel did not — it was Gary Moore's "I've Got A Secret" show.

This man with a secret represented himself as a Christian gentleman, a Physical Scientist working in the field of "Electro-Dynamics." He was going to demonstrate to the audience that one could let 1,000,000 volts of electricity pass through the body without being harmed in the least. He was going to use his own body to prove it.

The panel, as might be expected, did not guess his secret. First the demonstrator requested those on the stage to stand well back from the devices.

You may well know he didn't have to repeat the request. Then, he stepped to the larger of the two devices and turned a knob. Instantly, long tongues of livid electrical flame shot from the top of the smallest of the two cabinets . . . 1,000,000 volts of it!

This was a visual demonstration of the passage of this tremendous voltage through these cabinets. Then, turning it off, he explained that turning the other dial one degree would change the cycle — not the voltage, just one point; thereby conforming to the law of Electro-Dynamics, which would permit the passage of this tremendous voltage through the human body without injury to the cells whatever. He further explained that without this certain knowledge of how the law works, the results would be fatal.

Now the Scientist stepped over to the smaller of the two cabinets and mounted the top of it from a chair placed beside it. He had a board or paddle about three inches wide and about three feet long in his hand. He had previously said that this board would be burned to a cinder in the demonstration. Then he asked Gary Moore to turn the smaller of the two knobs on the large cabinet one point. This Gary did. Instantly the sound of the passage of high electrical voltage was plainly heard. The demonstrator recoiled downward about a foot and the paddle began to burn. It seemed at least a minute of this but probably was no more than thirty seconds. Then Gary turned off the current either by signal or prearranged plan. I doubt if anyone observing this demonstration was unconvinced.

This illustration should make it clear to anyone that ignorant misuse of this or any Universal Law excuses no one regardless of their moral status in life.

In physics every one accepts the authority and efficiency of these known Laws. This cannot be said of the higher Spiritual Laws, which are no less infallible. Why should one neglect to regard *them*, at least, as seriously? Is this not tragic? Has not this fact resulted in a confused fearful society searching for some way out of its dilemma — before disaster strikes?

We have been dealing with the basic Laws of life in this treatise, endeavoring to point out *"First Cause"* for the apparent tensions that are boiling to the explosive point around the world.

Whether one is a conscientious God-fearing person — a staunch church-goer or the man of the street, so to say, he or she looks to some established authority for guidance. So, I ask, "What Authority"?

The significant lesson to be learned here in this demonstration of the efficiency of physical laws is, that no matter how innocent one is, in a moral sense — a violation of this Electro-Dynamic Principle on the part of the user would be fatal.

How much more or less does reason permit us to regard the importance of the higher rules of life? After all, the "Discoverer," (Science) has been guided in the direction of its discovery by adhering particularly to the Principle of "Evolutionary Progress" — the Principle that has so signally been disregarded in the department of moral education.

The Scientist says to the aspirant of his particular field of endeavor: "Learn and adhere" to the laws of Physics and in so doing, *prove* them for yourself." The Sage in his moral teaching says the same thing of the higher Laws. He voices no objection to dogmas — only when their precepts do not coincide with Universal Principles. How can anyone who thinks seriously believe the world's troubles can be solved in any other way than getting in rapport with Universal Laws as we *Know* them to be?

How many of us regard the term Principle as something one can set up for himself? It is true man can set up rules for himself but Universal Principle was here before man, the earth or the Universe was in existence — these are Eternal.

Ideologies change their concepts when they are forced to, by public pressure, but the Principles they have been interpreting *never change*. The climactic struggle between materialism and its associated popular beliefs and the higher Spiritual Creative Laws, which are shedding their light on mankind at this moment in history as never before, cannot be resolved short of a clearer concept of the Laws we are dealing with.

This cusp of change, from what we call the Aquarius Age to that of the Pisces Age, has been prophesied exactly by the immutable Divine Laws this writer has been endeavoring to explain.

If "Racial-thinking" has by the Principle of Cause and Effect, (Divine Justice) brought the world to what it is today — pray where, if not in the "Originating Cause" — (or the way we think) are we to tackle the problem?

From the cradle to the grave we all are being guided by our acceptances, be they true or false. Just as fast as a *sincere* person learns that what he or she has been believing in has turned out to be false, and renews their convictions to conform to the new light, would not only be the part of wisdom, but the only way under Heaven that man can place himself in harmony with God's Law of *Evolutionary Progress*.

This is the same as saying that there is no escape for any of us from the eventuality of adhering to this Law. To say that there is, is a denial of the self-evident fact that evolutionary Progress is responsible for the differences in the world we live in today, and that of the year One.

It is true that most of us take two steps forward and slip back one, simply because we cannot build a positive consciousness in a day. New concepts are paid for in the "Coin of the Realm" or mental effort — supported by physical action, in a relaxed faithful atmosphere. The new and better life is free to anyone who will open their mental doors to the *spirit* of Truth.

Most followers of the Christian philosophy, though firm believers in a Divine Spiritual Standard, have been and are more and more puzzled over two terms; they are the theories around which our moral society accepts as authority and upon which the Master's teaching rests. They are called "Grace and Truth." Of course, ordinarily, we understand that Truth and Reality are perfect synonyms. And that a wrong construction placed on the meaning of Grace would lead us to infer that one can be relieved of their responsibility regardless of Divine Laws, which obviously are standards for *all* mankind.

Was it not the Church's authority concerning the meaning of Truth, that Jesus challenged in His day? — and which culminated in His death on the Cross?

The centuries have slowly brought about clearer light upon the truths of the Master's teaching more among independent seekers out of the Church than in it. Isn't this but the operation of the Principle of Evolutionary Progress? Why should we not recognize this Progressive Principle in the realm of morals — the realm of Christianity? It isn't displacing Christian Principles but coming to higher understanding of them.

Psychologists can explain away the reason people are not only passively reluctant to face long-held convictions, but will even murder in defense of them.

Over forty years of search for a cohesive rationalization

of these inconsistencies in our interpretation of Reality have brought radical changes in the pattern of the writer's thought. I am certain I have not retrogressed — this I have proven thousands of times for myself.

I have no doubt that temperatures will rise, even in this late day, when reading this seemingly unpalatable challenge to centuries-old beliefs. It was that way with me — I am thankful my mind was not completely closed.

This is only normal human behavior. It is the way the mind works — It is the way we grow in evolution. We fear the dark of the unknown — until the light of reason dissipates the darkness, then we recognize the blessing that has been there all the time just waiting for us to recognize and understand.

It is said that one is saved by "Grace". How reliable is our authority? Do we divide the authority between the Holy Bible and the Dictionary? Are they in conflict?

The dictionary defines Grace as: "Any excellence; characteristic attraction or endowment; elegance of action or language; beauty or embellishment."

The same dictionary defines the orthodox religious interpretation of Grace as: "The unmerited favor" and love of God toward man in Christ; Divine sanctifying, regenerating and preserving influence; Spiritual excellence or virtue." Do you see any discrepancy in these statements of accepted authority? Does one attain excellence of character outside the progressive Laws of God which we call Divine Principle? Is our Spiritual Father capable of changing the nature of His Divine Being to fit any case what-so-ever and still never "Cast a shadow of turning" — and still be unprejudiced?

If the faculty of reason God gives us can accept the Principle of an inflexible God-Law-Character, how, at the same time, can we accept any orthodox theory indicating man can be excused from his ignorant or wilful misuse of unchangeable Universal Law, as "unmerited favor" would indicate — and still believe we think for ourselves?

As will be recognized, the whole question revolves around whether or not there is an erroneous concept of the Master's plain teaching, which is: that *faith* in the *power* of *"Divine Laws"* can build Divine Characters in human Beings — *when practiced.*

When "lip service" gives way to sincere effort to learn and practice the Principles, then we may begin to see life take on a higher meaning — a happier sequence of events.

The reason our prayers are not answered may not be apparent to a casual observer. On a deeper search we find that somewhere along the soul's journey the necessity of keeping the Law was not yet clear and made a matter of practice progressively speaking.

So, rest assured that our inability to find a cause is not a contradiction of the immovability of Universal Laws. The maturing of a soul's understanding takes more than one mere "class room" in a material body. Mental and spiritual progress is a necessity under Universal Law. There is no substitute for understanding.

Orthodoxically approved good Christians or our innocent children have not in all history escaped penalty or reward when due under Universal Divine Law.

There comes to mind an incident in my childhood days; a group of us boys were playing "follow the leader"; we came to a hundred and fifty-foot steel frame tower used to light the city of Council Bluffs, Iowa. All but my friend, Hogy, and I had dropped out when it came to climbing that tower.

We climbed to the top of it and it looked like my friend and I would break even. Until I, in my determination to out-banner my competition, decided to "hand-over-hand" out on a steel guide-wire slanting to the ground about forty-five degrees from where it was fastened to the tower, twenty-five feet from the top.

I hadn't a thought of the hazard involved until I came to getting back from where I was hanging, about ten feet out away from the tower. The slant of the cable necessitated pulling myself up as well as moving towards the tower.

I hadn't thought of that possibility in my enthusiastic determination to out-banner Hogy.

Panic struck me when I had reached a couple of feet from the tower — my strength was taxed seemingly to the limit. I *realized* for the first time my perilous position.

"Something" gave me the added strength I needed. For some time I clung to the upright steel pipe to which was fastened the cable and on which was threaded the ladder — like steps to the ground.

This experience afforded a lesson I had to learn. It was a point in the evolution of my soul. It had a purpose in the education of a soul — it was a blessed event that in the nature of things had to take place. A prayer was uttered, a response was forthcoming because I had *learned my lesson;* perhaps the hard way, but nevertheless I had then and there realized the danger of ignorantly playing around with the Principle of Gravity. I could just as easily have ended my days this time around if my number had been up, but the time was not just right — I had a lot more to learn in life's short span and besides I was only beginning in this classroom.

This chapter is intended to specifically point out a centuries-old error in religious teaching that has misled millions of sincere people into the false hope they can saddle their conscious or unconscious behavior, good, bad or indifferent, on any agency other than themselves.

In explaining this tragic discrepancy let us again remember the "Christ of God" is the dynamic phase of God in man — the I Am — the verb to be — the Lord God —

the Giver of the Law. I am reminded of a line in one of the Christian hymn books that runs like this: "Take it to the Lord in Prayer." Do we realize that every question, desire or animosity is taken to that "Monitoring Conscience" which is the Christ and Lord God, the spirit of Truth at the center of our consciousness?

Any favor or salvation, by whatever name it is called, can be but a *result* of keeping the law, which is: "As a man thinketh in his heart (or deeply) so is he" — and *what* he is, that is, in his *convictions*, that, and nothing more, does the outer world reflect back to him. In short, man *merits* exactly what he, himself, has initiated *by Law;* not "unmerited favor." Man has to learn and earn his position and responsibility in the Divine plan of Creation.

Have you seen children behave like little beasts and have said so at the time? Of course you have. At times they all do. They do so because they have not learned their responsibility before the Laws of life. Adults are only grownup children that have rightly or wrongly been instructed. Conscious life is a classroom in which much of our learning depends upon our teachers. In scientific fields *"Progress"* as a Principle is highly recognized. In the orthodox moral areas stagnation persists. Are not effects always in strict relation to *First Cause?* Ask yourself. Are there any more deserving of a temporary suspension of Divine Laws than innocent children? Jesus said of the children: "Of such as these is the kingdom of heaven." These children's reactions to life will follow along what they have been taught and the sins of the forefathers will be visited upon them unto the third and fourth generations. Do you still wonder why the innocent still have to suffer? — where the responsibility of teachers rest?

Grownups, more often than not, are stuffed with intellectual learning, but still ignorant of the Divine moral requirements of Universal Law.

Do you, the reader, object to these statements of Divine Law? Would we have world-wide confusion and its tensions today had mankind been taught the real facts concerning these unbreakable rules of life? Denoninational moral teaching has been with us for centuries, with little progress in their concepts of Truth, until recent years. The writer is caught up in the vanguard of this "New Light" — It has revolutionized some of his fond concepts, too. It has been made so clear to him that it is hard to understand why it is that some others find his explanations so difficult to understand.

In ancient times education was for the privileged few. Today, for the most part, it is free, except in the advanced phases. And here, as most of us know who have grown youngsters going to college, it takes money, which infers there are still restrictions in an economic sense. Again the point of error shows up with emphasis. Which of these departments of education have failed to progress? Not physical Science — not in economic or social communication, except, in the moral quality of these departments . . . so again the finger points to that moral department which should *guide* in the *right use* of the products of these other departments.

It is understood that Grace and its relation to instantaneous healing is a paramount question in the mind of one trying to rationalize new and unfamiliar concepts of God's Laws.

The graduation of the human race from the Nomadic to an Agrarian society is progress in action just as Christianity brought revolutionary ideas of man's relationship to God; or when Henry Ford introduced a new principle into manufacturing methods and the end-purposes of industrialism — from the idea of profits as a primary motive to service *to all* with profit but a by-product. Every one knows Ford was beset with lawsuits by the old established "pace-setters" — they resisted the new idea despite Ford's successful demonstration that a greater degree of service to the whole brought incontestable proof that in this new and strange principle's wake came profits far outstripping his more static competitor's dreams. *Evolutionary progress,* as principle, is demonstrated in both the moral and the physical departments in these above facts.

One may be wondering if Instantaneous Healing is a true *fact* of the life processes. The answer is yes, but it isn't sidestepping the Law, as "unmerited favor" indicates. However, it *is* "Instant Illumination" of the individual mind — it can apply in a specific sense or in a general prayer for understanding, i.e. — understanding of man's relationship to Divine Being. In an instant we are raised from darkness to light — from disease to health — always *in our mind first.* The effect of this Light quickly shows forth outwardly.

When we keep the faith with this new knowledge it becomes a habitual pattern of thought. If we permit ourselves to drop back into old habits we, of course, again succumb to our former troubles. This is what Jesus meant when He said: "Thy sins are forgiven, *go thou and sin no more."* It is open-minded *acknowledgment* and acceptance *without question,* of the *Power,* behind God's Word, which implies faith. It is the *Power* that is channeled through the *dynamic phase* of His Being (The Christ) that heals and maintains one in mental and physical health. We may call this "Unmerited favor" but again, it is a *merited keeping of the Law.*

And now we come to an equally erroneous concept of the meaning of *Reality.* Again the great majority accept the standard Dictionary as the authority. Webster's Dictionary defines Reality as: Actual existence; fact; truth; reason; the existence of a mental faculty which enables man to deduce inferences from facts: to distinguish right from wrong; efficient or final cause; right judgment; cause for opinion or act; infer conclusions from an argument.

Before anything can exist, the *soul* of it must exist. For the soul of it *embodies* the idea and purpose *of* it. It follows then that ideas are always abstract in essence. To many, reality is confined to something that is *manifest* to the *physical* senses — It must be of a psychological or material nature in order to be considered real.

Now what the dictionary is saying is that *facts* are but *effects* of reality; the truth or evidence that something *really exists*. Inferences; right judgment; conclusions and opinions are all *ideas* in the mind and mind is, itself, Life — not material — not gray matter. The only way yet discovered to handle abstract ideas is mentally — that is, by the character or essence, or spirit that composes the idea.

We live among things and conditions of our own concept of them and the concept of them is never *identical* to another human being's idea of them. ONLY the Christ's idea of them remains identical with *every other soul's living Christ Principle*. The existence of anything is the reality of it, which again, is embodied in the idea of it. It is purely a mental concept and must, as a consequence, be evaluated metaphysically. Without an idea of it, no thing can exist in consciousness. By the same token — Divine Mind, or Substance, out of which all things are made, is pure Light, ("The Father of Lights"). It can and does exist without one's being aware of It. Substance, Spirit or Divine Mind has always existed.

Man is but an instrumentality for the expression of ideas in the all-imaginative Mind of God, which includes the mind of the individual. This means that reality only exists in the Mind of God in the form of ideas, which we are wont to call our own when they appear in our mind.

When we accept or appropriate another's ideas, a change takes place in our own world; in degree it is unlike the ones we have held. The flow of ideas into the individual's mind never ceases nor is it static or progress in some degree could never be. Herein lies the great responsibility of a teacher — a "way shower". Jesus was but a Way Shower who had reached the ultimate measure of the Christ of God within Him. That point of perfection was marked in history by "Calvary's Cross". That event was not a sacrifice but an attainment of perfection by the *human* Jesus who said, himself, or in words to the same effect, "Do not as I do, but as I say". The sense of this statement is that no two or more souls are created for identical purposes. The Divine Plan calls for a multiplicity of purposes. Calvary's Cross outpictures the finish of a process — that of bringing the Father (Divine Mind), the Son, (The dynamic phase of Divine Mind), and the Holy Spirit — the Trinity's three points, together into a perfected instrumentality of the Divine Creative Plan.

The soul of Jesus, which I have said before, was cast in Eternity for a specific purpose in the Divine Plan just as are you and I. Jesus had lived on the material plane in other personalities before. Our Bibles tell us that, too. He became one with the Christ of God on this earthly culminating "time around" *in progression.* In *His* purpose as a *perfected* Way Shower, His "Second Coming" is now in progress in the nature of a Divine Spiritual understanding, which comes "stealing" into the minds of men and women who have made themselves receptive — who have resisted the shackles of erroneous dogma that have for hundreds of years been forging the chains of *restrictive thinking* around the human race — *not* the freedom that Jesus was called to teach, which belongs to us all.

The governor and stabilizer of right relations rests with the teachers and leaders of the churches of the world. If they be blind to the facts of Reality (Truth), their sheep will surely fall in the abyss of turmoil, confusion, suffering and death in the present world. Say you not this is true?

These are stakes we risk in this day of the New Age.

In speaking of Christendom, we are speaking and including the high offices of the countries of the world. They all spring from some traditional religious belief which has changed little since its inception.

If the reader is not ready for these revealing truths he or she will know, for they will be resented. That *is* as it *should be* under the Principle of Progression. The minds of mankind are not constructed to be able to assimilate new ideas in one gulp. In the early stages of human progression man learns by trial and error. Later along the soul's progressive journey he begins to listen to the inner conscience for guidance. This is not new; we have but to look with seeing eyes.

The urge to know keeps pace with the assimilation of each lesson as it comes. A lesson is an experience — bless them regardless of how cruel they may be, for they represent something the soul must learn.

The truth or falsity of a teaching must show up in the acid test which encompasses the following question: Does a credence, dogma or interpretation coincide with Universally known and established Divine Laws, or can one find a divergence — an incompatibility — an inconsistency, or an outright contradiction? If there *is* such an inconsistency, this fact (evidence of existence) is proof of an error in understanding. Concepts based on Truth or Reality have their reward through the Principle of Divine Justice (cause and effect) — though we have believed it to be an unwarranted stepping out of character by Divine Justice.

The reader will no doubt want to know what happens when one transfers his or her allegiance to know established Principles — when one comes to a higher light than that held previously and unprogressively through a lifetime. Do they lose anything of superior value?

Perhaps the writer can best answer that question by referring to his own experience. With me, a conflict began between subconscious acceptances of long standing and the reasoning faculty of the conscious mind. Reason won out, and a new and fantastic but soul-satisfying vision of the rightness — the justice, and a solid foundation of real Christian Principles, in relation to the time-tested Laws of Life, has emerged. There had always been something missing — something that didn't "hold water" (hold thought), an incomplete circle, which didn't make sense. I have had to accept what others in authority have counseled, even though they could not explain the contradictions that existed in their teachings. Now I feel perfectly secure — I have a standard that answers the whys and wherefores direct from the Source of all wisdom — in exact relation to my *Human progressive ability* to interpret Wisdom's promptings. I have found freedom from fear — I have found a higher concept of love for my fellowmen — a charity towards victims of erroneous teaching — not the kind of charity that holds the needy in the limitations they would escape from. But the kind that would help them to help themselves.

For the most part, food for the body is quickly dissipated — but food for the mind and soul that is tinctured with the truth of Life is an ever-growing strength, peace, and sense of security that never, never fails no matter what the winds of ignorance and strife and tension generate. These values were never forthcoming in my allegiance to orthodox interpretations of Christian Philosophy.

I know in my heart, now, why I teetered between the *Spirit* of the Christian Principles and the "letter" of them. And I know now that every human being must come to learn and know the true relationship they, as human individuals, bear to their Divine Creator. And why this is uncontradictably so. I know that the powerful urge that was born in my mind and heart to know the Truth of Life over sixty years ago, was far from being accidental — much less the multiple times I have been saved from disaster.

Looking back on my own pathway and the hard lessons

I had to learn, they have now been revealed as blessings in disguise. I wouldn't trade my health and happiness for all the wealth in the world — for I have found that material wealth, more often than not, has brought unhappiness instead of the peace of mind which the seeker erroneously, via money, has sought.

Oh no, I've not thrown out the Christian Principles — only the wrong concept of them. I am not offering an easy panacea — I have and am now, paying for every thing of value this world of experience has to offer — "in the coin of the realm". Just so does the reader, though he or she may not be aware of it. But I have also found — the payments become easier and even joyful as time passes.

Many that are blessed with advantages such as physical and mental equipment, birth and economic position, do not realize or appreciate how fortunate they are. The easy acquiring of an education and understanding is construed as license to many, to vainly lord it over others. Human vanity is a poor substitute for pride of Spiritual understanding. Destiny, however, is forever striking a balance. Every soul must learn this sooner or later. This I know from experience; for, as a boy of thirteen, I was out around the world learning the hard way. At eighty-eight, I am "at peace with the world and mankind", as the lyrics of a popular song go. The hills were mountains in those days and the valleys deep. How marvelously they have leveled off. Not by accident — not because of luck — but because of what I know now to be the keeping, as best I can, of the Divine Rules of Life, I have become more in harmony with them in my daily thoughts and acts. Not that there isn't a lot still to be desired. The way ahead reaches out to Infinity. But of this I am assured — I am progressing in the right direction with all the authority I am worthy of — and in the name of our Spiritual Father — "I" am pointing the way to all who will L—i—s—t—e—n.

DETAILED DESCRIPTION OF THE

CREATIVE PROCESS

The circle has always symbolized the area of consciousness, whether the unlimited mind of God or the limited, of mankind which is on the progressive pathway to becoming the likeness of the Father.

The symbolic plate on page 182 does two things — first, it shows how the Divine Mind of God (the large A) is eternally present in the conscious and subconscious minds of mankind, as well as the "instinctive life of the animal". Secondly, it shows how the hand of God most assuredly guided the architect in the inconceivable task that went into the building of the ancient Egyptian Pyramid, Cheops.

By following my instructions, I am sure you will agree why physical science is puzzled as to how, in the category of physics, this monumental task was accomplished. Trying to prove spiritual methods of discernment by limited physical standards is not in keeping with the higher echelon of Spiritual Law.

Now please note — there are seven small circles representing the seven cosmic days of the Creative Process through which mankind must pass before he can qualify as an image of his Creator.

The first day represents the initial idea in Divine Substance of God Mind which is still, static and in perfect balance. "B" represents the field of human awareness. The "Cross bars, C" represents the Dynamic Phase of the Father — or the Son — the Light — the Word — the Christ — which at this point is still, quiet and balanced and in the Father's House, so to speak.

The small "A" at the intersection of these "Christ Cross Bars" becomes the Dynamic Phase of the "Word" or

Christ or Lord God and continues to hold this position through the Creative Process.

The second day circle is represented as a gaseous or imaginative period when the idea of mankind's purpose in the Mind of God takes place in life expression.

Third day circle stages the beginning of the elemental support called the chemistry of nature, represented by another circle within the outer circle indicative of the "mineral kingdom".

The fourth day follows with an added circle representing the "vegetable kingdom".

The fifth day ushers in the "animal kingdom", initiating the "animal Body-abode" in which the surmounting human Being with a Divine Soul is to function on the material plane.

The sixth day circle represents the first appearance of the "Human Being" called "man", whom, by the way, Scriptures indicate did not appear to the eye until a suitable physical body had been built up to contain his soul on the material plane. This juncture in the process initiates the soul's ascent in building the twelve faculties of his mental equipment. Also, at this point, ushers in the significance of Egypt's Pyramid Cheops, called the "Bible in Stone", which strangely coincides with my concept of the Creative Process above it on this same page. But my purpose here is to point out briefly the significance of its outline.

The ground surface base is what greets the eye, but below the surface lie six levels that coincide with my concept of the Creative Process. And, please, may I remind the reader that I am the writer but the "author" is beyond the ken of the five physical senses.

Without this inspirational guidance I could not have survived these eighty-eight years, much less communicate the Truth this message contains. I feel this message is the unfinished business that keeps me here — and in the face of events — it is needless to point out — It is timely.

A FEW AXIOMS OF PRINCIPLE

On page 184 the symbol of our Solar Orb graphically portrays how all living things in nature are not only supported, but identified mathematically by number and rate of the billions of single vibratory rays of the Sun. Not one atom that finds its way into the world of matter is unaccompanied by Divine Intelligence at its center.

It provides the instinct that motivates the limited consciousness of animal life. Mankind has a plus of the same ingredient.

The seat, or soul-idea — like the center of a cyclone, is always perfectly still no matter the turmoil that surrounds it. Our Father-God is in perfect balance, which means He is still, cold and silent. Heat comes from cold — not the reverse. "Backtrack" the colors of the spectrum and they turn out to be perfect white. At the center of our Solar Orb rests the White Light of God. The Master, Jesus, speaking in the consciousness of the Christ within said, "I am the Light that lighteth every man that cometh into the world" and "I will be with you always". Always is not limited to the life of this world, nor was He speaking of the nature which the Solar Orb supports, but rather the Christ Presence that indwells us all.

CHAPTER IX

BUILDING A NEW OUTLOOK

"Desire" is an urge to possess. Desire for something always precedes the will to possess it. A desire to possess is not compatible to unreceptivity; therefore, the very first condition of the individual mind must be receptivity supported by the will to make use of any principle necessary to the end in view. Principles, though abstract, are the firmest of all foundations. This must be understood for it is the very procedure required to attain an understanding of any theory of whatever nature.

The *desire* to understand more about life did not begin with the "outer" you. Habits of thought will resist tenaciously new ideas, especially if they be contrary to what you have believed. Understanding of the way the mind works every psychologist knows. We see it proved out in the *progress* of physical science every day. By the same token, we see the lack of progress in understanding in the religious institutions of the world. You, yourself, would no doubt not be interested in reading this book if you were wholly satisfied in your understanding of life.

The circumstance which initiates a desire comes in millions of ways — always in the nature of an idea or light. The *way* is un-important. But *the urge is.*

If there was nothing to be gained in understanding by conscious mind, maintaining the concentration of the will never would have happened. Nothing is accidental in this Universe of Cause and Effect.

Acquainting one's self with the way the mind works is a requisite to higher understanding. A strong desire or will is also a requisite.

Distinguishing the departments of the Conscious and the Sub-Conscious Mind, is still another requisition. The Sub-Conscious picks up the impressions the imagination exhibits. It is the link between the pattern in the imagination and the outer manifestation of an idea. In other words, if the idea impressed upon the Sub-Conscious is "understanding" — understanding eventually becomes a *possession* of the conscious mind. Maintaining the concentration of the will upon a given subject, such as understanding and a sense of knowingness or knowledge of the Truth.

Further along I shall explain how one may, through exercise of the concentrative powers of the mind, develop rapidly the mental grasp and understanding of Universal Principles. This phase must precede the *spiritual knowledge* of constructive living. Also, this is the one and only solution to Universal peace that must, by its very nature, precede in the hearts and minds of the individual first before peace may reign on this troubled earth. And this, too, is what the Master Jesus voiced in His day as He listened to the guidance of the Christ Spirit within Him.

The great majority of us will complain of world problems. There are many who will endeavor to come up with patent answers to them. If the answers arrived at are hard to take, we usually think it is the other fellow that needs the guidance.

This is not uncommon. We all have at one time or another been afflicted with an exaggerated purity complex in religious matters.

The writer also offers his views of the situation. The strength of his convictions must rest upon *known* Universal

Laws: not some obvious unprovable theory. Those "known" Universal standards, which when understood rightly, have never in all history failed to operate in exact relation to every other *known* Universal Principle.

One should never be afraid to trust his all to Universal Divine Laws because of any inability to define the power that results prove exists. Those principles we have come to accept unquestionably, we do not fear. Furthermore, we *know* that unless we bring our lives in rapport with the the nature of these Laws, we do not get the desired results, though we may think we do at the time, and this holds true whether one be a brilliant intellectual or unable to write his own name.

So, to begin with, we must learn to mentally "Listen".

Pure open-mindedness is a rare characteristic which is understood. But, if one can accept the Master's word on the way Divine Laws work, in *every* condition, then it will be easier to understand that our first concern in matters of religion is to think of God as Law. That, when broken up into His "component parts," He is *all the Principles.* And, furthermore, we must remember that *if* a principle *is* a principle, it can never vary one infinitesimal iota in performance.

Jesus is purported to have said, "Except ye become as little children, ye can in no wise enter the kingdom of heaven." He was no more speaking of some place off in the sky than He was speaking of acquiring a new set of brains when he gave us to understand that one must *renew his mind* to grasp the Truth.

Mental receptivity is a first requisite to understanding and understanding is a pre-requisite to unimpeded progress.

Of course the kingdom of heaven is a state of awareness of Truth and Truth *is* Reality and a consciousness of Reality results in a harmonious life when lived in accordance with *Divine* purpose.

Jesus' authority stands out again when He said, "Know ye not the kingdom of heaven is within you." Or when He said, "Know ye not ye are Gods" and that "I (God) will be with you always."

Also, it is understood that the statement, "Ye must be born again" is allegorical but how do *you* interpret the underlying spirit of this parable? However, when we realize the term "water" as used so often in the Bible means "Thought" and "Seas" mass thought, we will find these terms where used, in relation to the context, is perfectly reasonable and scientifically logical and do not contradict that statement so often misinterpreted: "In the beginning was the "Word" and the Word was *with* God and the Word *was God*"! The term "Word" as used here is a *"thought"* or an *"idea"* or a *"light"*.

When we receive a thought or an idea or a light in our mind, we are wont to call that idea ours. A little thought about this and we will find the idea we called *ours* is, in the last analysis, not really ours at all. For there is only One Power that can think which is the same as saying that *All* ideas come from the *Same Source*, namely, "Divine Intelligence".

So here on the best of authority, you may feel perfectly secure in laying aside any preconceived notions, at least till you have digested the message contained herein.

The nations of the world are grasping for straws and no pun intended when I say some of these straws may hold great promise, if we will look into them guided by Divine Law — not hearsay.

And now, if our mental doors are at least a little ajar, let us note the Principle upon and around and through which all things must evolve: psyche or material. It is called the *"Creative Principle"* — the only Creative Principle or *First Cause* provable in the experiences of mankind.

The Sages of the Far East knew of this Principle ages

ago. (The Bible symbolizes the same thing when it tells of the "Three Wise Men" that came to the Truth.) Their explanation is wrapped in mystery for most Westerners. The writer will endeavor to clarify the intrinsic import it bears upon world conditions today — as well as in all past history.

So again, let us reiterate: *First Cause or the Creative Principle is* "Thought", "Idea", or "mental illumination".

Before we can be conscious of anything in the world, we must *have* the idea in the mind. The first conception of a thought is the *"Beginning"* of creation in the individual's world of experiences. Man has no power of *his own* to think and, it follows, to create. Man thinks he thinks. It will be seen that whatever manifests in this visible world is due to the twisting of *pure ideas* to conform to man's limited understanding through the power of choice he is endowed with.

The outpicturing of thought manifests in many degrees. The thoughts most potent in manifestation are those in our *deep convictions.* A strong conviction results in definite objectification. Weak convictions, or more wishful thinking, objectifies in kind, degree for degree. Man is responsible for his world by the Law of Creative Cause, and not by traditions, where tradition contradicts the *Reality* of the *Creative Principle* above mentioned.

When the term truth is used, it means Reality of Divine Universal Law, not the *manner* in which it is used or the defining of Itself. No man can define God except to say God is Law and Law "never casts a shadow of turning".

If the reader can accept the above explanations, let us proceed to the next Principle — *"Effect"*, which we define here as that which results from Cause. There can be no effect without an adequate Cause and there can be no adequate Cause without an idea, thought, or light.

Now we come to the actual process. Here is where we

take a closer look at that *faculty*, that *tool* that so many think is so unreliable because they see so many playing games with it — "Imagination".

Imagination is the tool, the faculty, the medium, the canvas upon which the *artist's conception* of an idea takes on a nebulous form. If an idea, regardless the end in view, is indefinite, uncertain or changeable, it is clearly prophetic of what the effect will be by the time nature's chemistry brings it into view to the physical senses.

Your world, as mine, we have *thought into being*. If we were not responsible, we could not be conscious of it. If we deeply believe it is unreal, it is unreal, *to us*. If we blame our teachers, whether facts point to their responsibility or not, it is we that have been given freedom of choice to erase any error a teacher may have implanted in our minds by acceptance.

It is clear how much a teacher may, through lack of understanding of the Divine Laws, impede the progress of those he is teaching. The responsibility of his calling is greater and therefore focuses the great need for correction. This, in a word, is what this book is all about.

The Master Jesus was first of all a teacher. He was the "Way Shower" — not one that could relieve man of his responsibilities under the Law. His wisdom and strength was His knowledge of the Laws. He taught Divine Principles, not panaceas. Panaceas are but escape methods for man's responsibilities under Law.

Those of us who cling to ancient panaceas are merely delaying our *progress*. So we come to the stumbling block of Orthodox Christendom. "Progress" is a Universal Principle which is basic to the Creative Principle. Without progress there can be no life. Progress is not confined to any one department of life. Conforming to progress is responsible for the great strides physical science is making around the world. The lack of this principle shows up with terrific foreboding in the most important department of life — the "Moral". The moral department is the most important because it is the guiding factor in the constructive use the ingenuity of human endeavor is being put!

There is no need to overemphasize the rapid trend toward self-destruction the world of science and invention is plunging the human race — unbridled by moral consideration.

We blame Russia for her ungodliness because the church is nearly non-existent in her land. But we of the West are building armaments like mad! Armaments that when activated are capable of snuffing out the lives of millions, just as well as the Russians. Are these armaments being built by non-believers in religious principles? Or only by those who do not recognize our common God?

Yes, Russia has given the church a bad time but they, no more or less than we of the West, can escape the consequences of our *convictions* — except by changing the pattern of our thoughts concerning *Reality* (Truth).

The large question of connecting up our own responsibility for things that happen to us lies in our inability to look beyond the horizon of this life's span. The only answer I've been able to accept lies within the scope of the principle we know as "Evolution". We think of evolution as dealing with manifest forms. The highest of which we know, or at least believe, is the *human organism*. But we lose sight of the life and light of the soul which looks out of your eyes and mine which is spiritual in essence and which we call the soul of man. This soul also lives under the Law of Evolution and which, necessarily, is under the *progressive* Principle.

It necessarily follows, the soul does not learn all of its lessons in one short span of life. Therefore, it can be readily understood that somewhere along his life's path of the soul, ignorance has sowed seeds of one kind or another that must work out under the Law of Cause and Effect which is not bound by time nor space. The Easterners call it "Karma".

Now the intelligence that brings one to accept these truisms is *knowledge of Universal Principles.*

I have been naming a few of the well-known Universal and therefore Divine Laws. Just a little consideration will convince the thoughtful person that a disregard for the Principle of "Progress" is a violation of Divine Law. The deep grooves of belief in erroneous religious teaching have closed many minds to even a consideration of what is written here. This is tragic. Closed minds believe there is something irreligious about progressive thinking when applied to spiritual matters of the church. Yet they readily grant it is all right in the physical world of effects. This, on the face of it, is a fallacy.

It may be said that the author of this message is taking a competitive view of the Christian teaching.

This, too, is not true. The principle of "Competition" is a law through which higher and still higher animal organisms are built up. The end purpose is obviously perfection. Where the same principle shows up in moral matters, the end purpose is likewise progress towards perfection in understanding the rules of life in accordance with Divine Purpose.

Always and forever evolutionary progression is clearly evident. Now, where do you stand in relation to this deep and undeniable Law of life (or law of *being*)?

Now we take up the Principle of "Cooperation: (to jointly work together for the same end).

When two or more people are joined together in common thought and endeavor in understanding Truth, they naturally rise above the law that rules in the lessor animal life ("Eye for an eye"). The difference between the "cooperation" expressed in the undisciplined in spiritual understanding shows up in such behavior as fighting one moment (so to speak) and loving the next.

The participants may or may not be mentally aware of the laws governing life but a deep religious conviction does not exist. A *being* which we understand to be true becomes our own only when we practice the principles. Once one lets this attitude of mind and heart become a habit though one is beset with all manner of trouble, he is miraculously given power to rise above them in mind and spirit. The peaceful mind attracts that which it is, in kind. So, first, a peaceful mind. A peaceful mind is a relaxed mind and a relaxed mind is more receptive to spiritual progress than one carrying a chip of doubt on its mental shoulder.

Which is it going to be? The justice and immovability of Divine Principles or a prejudiced God that had to be mocked by another power beside Himself . . . the "Devil" which Jesus said "was a liar and the father of it"?

Now, let us get together and begin to give our allegiance to Divine Principles. Not to a God way off in the sky. Not to a God that permits our innocent to perish in flames. Not to a God of precarious principles — that plays favorites — that permits selfish human prejudice outside the Law of Justice we believe Him to be. But let us give our all on the solid ground *that we* as images of Divine Principle are given all power in Heaven and in earth to use freely and without stint by learning and then acting in harmony with the Universal Laws of Divine Being. We must shoulder our responsibilities.

We have been given "freedom of choice". We have been endowed with intelligence to use — not a responsibility to saddle somebody else with. Those whose calling places them in the position of a "Way Shower" has a responsibility to learn the *Realities* of life, not the superstitions that have been handed down through the corridors of time to be perpetuated contrary to the basic and self-evident *Principle of Progress.*

Before the moral forces can exert influence on the purposes for which technological products are made, they must first discover where First Cause originates. For it is true that every psychological or physical effect that manifests in this world is, in the last analysis, but *transmuted* "Light" — or manifested ideas that emanate from thought.

BUILDING A NEW OUTLOOK
Part Two — Summary

Every happening in this Universe and of those millions of light years out in space stems from an idea in the Mind of God. If an idea can be imagined, it is possible. The Christian Bible says the same thing — "All things are possible to God."

The scope of this statement is as broad as the reaches of outer space or as Eternity Itself.

The Key to every mystery the world has ever been confronted with is within the grasp of every soul of mankind. The one and only condition that keeps him from solving every problem is lack of knowledge or ignorance — ignorance of the Laws of Being.

Note, I say "Being". Let us consider what the term implies. A clod is *being* a clod — a rock is being a rock — a tree is being a tree — a worm is being a worm — a rose is being a rose — a fish is being a fish and a man is being a man. As every possible idea must eventually become or *be* that for which it was conceived or nothing at all.

The first phase of the being of anything is a mental picture. The picture is purely abstract. One cannot *see* it with *physical eyes* or *touch* with *physical hands;* but one may feel or touch and mentally experience the idea by *discernment* or imagination.

All the marvelous creations of the times come about

within the strict organization of Divine Law — (God). I reaffirm, Divine Law is collectively, *all the Universal Principles*. Merely to think, we must make use of them, for thinking is creating. If without purpose, the fruits will be likewise, purposeless.

Flesh and blood or brains do not reveal the truth but the "Corner Stone", the fulcrum around which all creation revolves. The Spiritual Essence of all that is. Only in terms of Principles can the writer speak of these things.

The conception of any object or psychological condition is not the birth of it into manifestation, but its appearance in mind.

A desire becomes a picture in the mind first. The perfection of a picture in the mind requires concentrated attention. This is work but not labor if one's heart is in it. The strong urges we have, to know the truth, or to be free, are of Divine origin, just as is every thought we think, *at base*.

Those whose thoughts are constructive are the purest, or the nearest to Divine purpose. Man raises his human self towards the Divine pattern of God (Christ) within him, through *being* or practicing the Divine purpose for *him*. It is this Truth that underlies the Christian philosophy that makes it scientifically correct when understood rightly.

The reader that grasps the significance of the following principles and begins to place his or her thought processes in relation to them will find a new world opening up before them — a world of shrinking problems with his or her mental and spiritual feet planted on solid ground. The cause and the effects of world unrest and its prophetic import will no longer be a mystery.

Consider the chart of just seven of the Divine Laws on page 157.

May I suggest that the reader ask himself or herself: What is my 'thinking stance' with the foregoing truism in Mind? I believe the average person will come to realize with surprise, or perhaps chagrin, how the principle of cause and effect (Divine Justice) has and is bringing to to us penalty or reward for those things we, ourselves, have initiated by our creative thought processes.

As we downgrading this wonderful body mechanism of ours and getting a negative answer in experience? Or are we blessing it with the full knowledge that the Divine Creator's thought of it in the first place was one of perfection and that nothing short of the best possible abode should be the home of His Spirit — the "Christ Principle" — the "Guiding Principle" — our "Conscience".

Of course we, the souls of us, have to come to know the Truth by experience in many classrooms on this plane of matter. These consecutive classrooms reach back many generations. As the "Symbolic Plate" indicates — the Life Principle never for one moment deserts us, though many times we have thought It had. If such a thing were possible — the soul would have no Eternal verity — we could not exist!

We were meant to exist and we were given the faculties to discern this fact. How many times have I heard Dr. Frank Richelieu express the simple Truth, "There is not a spot where God is not." To the writer, he was saying: Where the Presence of Divine Intelligence is not. Be not deceived by appearances. When you go to bed at night, watch those thoughts in view of what you have hopefully learned in this message. Your subconscious, as such, is not examining them — it is just putting them into practice. If they were negative you will not have gotten the rest the mind and body needs. If they were constructive, you will arise with a zest to "get with it". Nothing but good can come from an understanding of the Science of Metaphysics.

The essence of the Master's teaching is not in conflict with the above message. Nor does the writer profess to be a worthy example of the principles he has come to acknowledge and teach. In this light I quote again, "He that is not against me is for me," or "Neither do I condemn thee, go and sin no more," or "He that has not sinned, let him cast the first stone." Carnal man is impeachable but God man is not.

These are the standards of understanding King Solomon thought should occupy first place in all our getting. They never vary from one Eternity to another or our Father God could be accused of casting a shadow of turning.

KNOWN UNIVERSAL LAWS VERSUS IDEOLOGICAL BELIEFS — YOUR CHOICE OF ALLEGIANCE

On pages 157-158 is a list of Universal Laws most people accept as unchangeable principles because throughout the records of history they have proven they are so.

Why should anyone desert their reliability as trustworthy guides for any limited human interpretation of what the Divine Laws of God are?

The writer is attempting to clarify the reason why and where the greatest error in human acceptances has shown up. The only way anyone can help another in spiritual matters is through relating the benefits of his own experience. This is showing the way — not doing the work each must do for himself.

Therefore, using the list of known principles stated, and referring to them by number, I will tell you why I have come to a conviction of the True Realities of life.

No. 1 — I believe that no one can honestly believe there is not an over-shadowing Intelligence of a spiritual nature behind the order of marvels in the Universe we live in. I believe this spiritual Intelligence which is everywhere present and in and through all, must *be all*. Being Spirit, It must operate through spiritual principles. Being the substance from which all manifestation springs, there must be some department of Its governing body of principles that controls the initial event of all manifestation. The Key that lead me to explore this question was the line in the Christian Bible that reads: "As a man thinketh in his heart so is he." To be conscious of anything whatever, requires thought. It follows one must live to think and all life is One Life. Man is a thinking creature, therefore, he must be an extension — not separate — from the Father Intelligence. Thought is composed of ideas and ideas are lights or illumination. Resolving God into Universal Spirit, He must be Pure Light (the light of the world). It follows behind and, in the last analysis, all things visible or invisible to the physical eye, is light. Since all things are resolved into light, then the moment this light ceases to exist, the visible world ceases to exist to that individual consciousness — extension of Divine Intelligence, "man". So, along this line of reasoning, I came to the conviction that "Thought or idea" (The Christian calls it the "Word of God".) is the initiator or Father, and sustainer of all creation. The question naturally follows: Did God through His extensions create also the ills of the world?

No. 2 — Thought, the Creative Principle. If man be an extension of the Father God, he must operate under and with the same freedom of choice as the Father Himself — being in His spiritual image. If the "image" lacks understanding, not having yet reached it by reason of his progressive position on the soul's evolutionary path of unfoldment, which is to be seen must take place under the evolutionary principle. Then, we have sufficient evidence from where the ills of the world must stem. In other words, they are the fruits of ignorance of the laws of life.

Also, when we observe the multitudinous forms these undesirable fruits assume from personal illnesses, negative superstitious teachings, sociological trends, political dishonesty, international tensions, wars, pestilences, poverty and distress and come to *realize* there is but one way possible these things could manifest, then and then only, can we be sure at which point a correction must be undertaken.

Just suppose the moral propagators of the Christian religion alone would have clearly understood and taken seriously the import of many clearcut statements their own "Text Book" makes regarding this tremendously important principle of Creation, such as where it reads in John (1.1, 14): "In the beginning was the Word and the Word was *with* God and the Word *was* God." It also explains, there is *nothing made* that *is* made except through this selfsame Word (meaning the thought or idea). This one passage of many is *all inclusive*. Should one limit this all inclusiveness in one infinitesimal degree, knowing a principle if it be a principle never varies in the least from one eternity to another, so to speak?

Now do you see as I do what gives rise to countless isms, dogmas, and cults of whatever nature which explains "Reality" in any other way that would shift the responsibility, or correction of man's ignorance and therefore, errors, to any other source than the mis-understanding *use* of this Principle of the Creative Process.

We would not think of expecting a right answer if we used the principle of numbers wrongly, because we do not question the authority of the purely abstract principle of mathematics. Then why adhere to unprovable theologies because they are traditional? Referring to No. 5 and No. 6 of the list where the combination of Evolutionary progress as principles are defined.

Should mankind disregard these Divine Laws as applying *only* to physical or material progression or the inclusion of all departments of being — especially the most important of all — the moral or spiritual department to which the church naturally belongs?

How can man expect to reap the benefits of keeping the Laws of God and single out any one of them to flaunt? Man is free to create any *panacea* or *escape* from responsibility and there is no question of a doubt the patronage, the various denominational creeds are enjoying, is due to just such practice.

As I see it, disillusionment is inevitable and the sooner it comes, the better for mankind. This I have proved in my own experience. I can only pass on this information. You must prove it for yourself.

Ideas in the mind must manifest in the world when supported by the will and conviction. Any letting down in will or conviction will delay or alter the outer effect as indicated by Principle No. 4 in the list. By the same token, the manifest world about us has and is being supported by the same Creative Process. If you like it, continue it in your thought patterns. If not, begin to discipline your thinking in terms of Universal Laws, rather than traditional beliefs.

The only life you *know* of is the one you are personally conscious of. Any other is a mere belief based upon appearances or what some one tells you. Any change in the picture must take place first in what you think of as *your* imagination. Somewhere along your path of unfoldment, you will find the "imagination", like your life, is in reality not yours, but exclusively the Divine Father's. Furthermore, I have found that every thought at its inception is pure. But by the time man's limited understanding interprets it, it might develop as anything but pure —hence, the impurities of the world.

No. 6 — The Competitive Principle belongs and is clearly operative in the lower strata of the creative process. Through the operation of this Law of survival, the animal organism in which the souls of men must function on this plane is brought to a required degree of perfection.

Once this required degree is attained, man enters a higher phase of his development. Higher mental and spiritual attainment is the purpose of a soul's calling, is a necessity before the soul, evolutionarily, can become a perfected extension capable of administering God's Laws according to the Divine plan. Jesus was a soul who had reached that degree, a perfected "Way Shower".

No. 7 — Signaling "finis", the day of rest, man's adulthood, is the era in which the Divine Spirit, the Holy Spirit, takes possession of the souls of men and which henceforth are controlled by the Cooperative Principle which we should note again means "To jointly work together for the same end". This higher principle is a Spiritual Law that in no way displaces the Animal Principle which will adhere so long as progress is a basic principle of the Creative Process.

If the two parts of this chapter fail to reach the mind of the reader at the time of reading, be informed that at some unsuspecting moment some truism written here will come winging its way into the mind with power and conviction, for the real author is none other than that perhaps undiscovered Self of you.

SEVEN OF THE UNIVERSAL LAWS GOVERNING THE DIVINE CREATIVE PROCESS

1. Divine Intelligence (Static Power)

   Law — Overall Principle — In and through All — Sustainer of All — Source of All — Life Principle

2. *Thought — Creative Principle* (Dynamic Power)

   First Cause — Principle of being through which all things come into being — Creative Thought, Word, or Christ Principle

3. *Imagination*   Nebulous state of *being* —
     (Spiritual appearance)   First stage of a manifesting idea.

4. *Manifestation*   Outpicturing — Objectification of an idea.
     (Physical appearance)

5. *Evolution*   Progressive chemistry of nature
     (Progression)

6. *Competition*   Animal Law of survival of the fittest.
     (Perfecting principle of nature)

7. *Cooperation*   Spiritual development of higher understanding and collective effort in the interests of Divine purpose — To jointly work together for the same end.

CHAPTER X

THE A B C's OF THE CREATIVE PRINCIPLE

By repetition of truisms in previous chapters, I have purposely brought the reader to this progressive point in the writer's interpretation of Reality. And now, with the guidance of the Divine Powers of Mind, I will proceed to put the A B C's of the Creative Principle in consecutive order, as God gives me the light to perceive them.

The reader, like many people, is searching for the mystical 'jewel of great price' promised in other terms throughout this book. Diamonds are seldom found on the surface — neither do the gems of truth always come without searching in the realm behind appearances. The nomenclature of the Creative Process boils down to comparatively few laws to remember.

Because it will be easier to understand the principles involved in our study, I will quote freely from a little booklet on thoughts for daily living by Dr. Frank E. Richelieu. No doubt it is the simplicity of his presentation of the workings of Principle in his writings and lectures that is bringing such a tremendous response from seekers of new concepts of ancient truths. But now let us go back to the Genesis version in the book of Moses in our Christian Bibles.

It tells us, "In the beginning — God". It is saying in reality there was no beginning without God. The authority for the truth as recorded in Genesis rests with Moses' interpretation, which must have been inspirational. The writer's authority for his attempt to rationalize whence and how Divine Being (God) had or had not an initial beginning, rests also with his inspirational guidance.

The feeling that comes to me is that 'space', understandably, had no beginning. It has always existed. The same must be true about God as the Spirit of Divine Mind must have infiltrated all space before anything at all could have come into being from a still or statically-balanced 'Mind-Intelligence'.

It logically follows, God had to initiate a dynamic phase of His statically-balanced Intelligent Power in order to activate His ideas. Thence comes His Creative Principle — the Christ Word of God or the Lord God which abides in us all as conscience or our moral sense. Along with the Creative Principle must come governing laws. The essence of Solomon's advice has to do with the laws of creativity. The creative power of thought issues from the indwelling Christ or creative thought-word which is an inner activity that is always creating something whether it be negative or constructive or positive or indifferent manner — as far as the individual is concerned.

That part of the Divine Mind called the Subconscious is in reality the dynamic phase of that which we call God. It is the 'Lord God'. Now let us build our structure of Divine Reality. God, variously called the 'Creator', the 'Father of Lights', 'Divine Mind', and many other appellations, is pure Spirit and is everywhere present (omnipresent) and in the last analysis comprises all that exists. Mankind's consciousness, for the most part, deals with the factual world of effects — therefore from appearances. We cognize our world as having a beginning and an ending — an inside and an outside. Factual cause is secondary cause, not the abstract First Cause.

Metaphysics opens the door to discerning Spiritual Causes. Ordinarily one does not understand why there is no outside to space, but we accept it. We do not understand why there is no beginning to God, or Divine Mind, but the Spirit of the letter back of the religious philosophies of the world is forever at One with the omnipresent Spirit of God.

So let us realize that God is Spirit and since there is no other 'real power' in existence He must be the Spiritual Substance from which all things are made that are made. Since the Divine Spirit which we call God must be in perfect balance or perfect stillness — from which all things come to exist — the underlying state of all ideas in the Mind of God is static — before they are activated by the 'word'.

Is it not clear that 'perfect balance' does not qualify if there is movement? It follows then, there must be a phase of God that is dynamic; that transposes the static idea into the realm of movement (creation). Now we come to the spirit of the statement that initiates our Holy Bible. 'In the beginning was the 'word' (Christ of God — the dynamic phase of the Father Himself) and the 'word' was God' . . . through which all things come into being and without which 'nothing is made that is made'.

In the last analysis, every vestige of all creation is and forever will be no more or no less than solidified Spirit. The 'letter' pictures the Creative Phase of God as the 'Christ of God' or the 'Lord God' or 'the Father's only Son' — 'His Creative Word' — the Spirit of which indwells us all as our conscience, which again lies at the very center of our consciousness — in particular, between the two lobes of our brain where our thoughts come from. This makes us all part and parcel of Divine Mind — for Life is One in whatever guise it appears.

As one looks out upon nature and its beauty with the

knowledge that the idea behind each of the atoms of matter that compose its appearance is centered with the indwelling Life Principle — how can one look at the intricate mechanism that composes our animal bodies and still question the subconscious functions of it as separate from the Life Principle? To do so would seem to me to be evidence of a need for the "renewing of our minds."

What we call our 'subconscious mind' is a wonderful gift to man. It is a servant — a link with the Creative Principle. It acts under the universal law of Cause and Effect. It does not question the validity of the thoughts we impress upon it. It is this truth that makes us responsible for what our convictions are. And let us not forget our indifferent surface thoughts also register in the outer world in degree of their strength.

Along with all creation come the Divine Laws that govern it. They are our 'true standards'. They are our refuge when we are confused. Because of the Progressive Principle, no one lives life without mistakes. It was the Master who said, "The poor will be with us always." This means the poor in understanding are coming into the world continually.

I repeat — our standards must be reliable, else we have no place to turn for guidance. Let us again be reminded all thought is creative of something. A thought' is an 'idea'. An idea lies back of every effect in the outer nature of materiality. The degrees of off-balance in our society today — as in any age of the past — is due to collective thinking.

Our lives become a comedy of errors when we try to change things from the standpoint of appearances. Clearly, this can never get the job done. This is the definite reason one must come to understand what discernment (metaphysical understanding) means. We must come to realize — there is the thinker but the thinker is not the thought.

The thinker drops the thought into the subconscious mind. Like the planting of a seed into the ground — the seed should be a good seed (constructive). The soil (creative law) must be watered and tilled (expectancy-faith). Here again 'water' in the Bible, interpreted, means thought and 'seas', mass thought.

God's intelligence is Spiritual — God's substance is Spiritual — God's laws are likewise Spiritual. So we must realize God's creations are Spiritual substance. I feel deeply that every out-picturing idea in the Mind of God is mathematically identified by a number and rate of vibratory impulses that compose it. I realize I am saying 'Nothing is outside the Spirit of God. Nothing is too insignificant. Nothing is imposingly unimportant.' What would happen if we ignored the insignificant principle of mathematics — the lowly digit? Many have tried to with negative results.

Many people question the principles voiced herein. They complain they have prayed and repeated constructive affirmations without results. Why? From long-standing convictions that they do not have the things or conditions they desire. It is a deeply subconscious conviction that must be reversed. When you pray for something in the Father's dynamic name, "I AM", which is the verb 'to be' — be that which you desire in your imagination (practicing the Presence) and you will have that thing or condition.

"It is the Father's good pleasure to give you the kingdom". "Know ye not the Kingdom of Heaven is within you?" Many parables of the letter of the Bible when interpreted spiritually have the answer to our questioning minds. There comes a time in the life of a soul when the convictions of which I speak here automatically become a stance in one's outlook — a continuing out-picturing prayer.

When the truth of the Twenty-Third Psalm, ". . . I shall not want . . ." becomes a living reality in the souls of mankind, then the so-called disciple has proven himself ready for the spiritual truths the Master, Jesus, (the Christ of God) came to teach. I have mentioned herein the importance of 'Divine Standards' for guidance. All of us will at times, under trying circumstances, get off the true progressive pathway, but we may quickly get back with 'true standards' for guidance. Though I have come to realize many spiritual truths in quite a long straightening path — I am still subject to some of the disturbing pressures that beset us. I find it most comforting that I can turn to true standards to get back on my progressive mental pathway.

And now, as a parting suggestion — if it has taken mass destructive thinking to bring the conditions we find so prevalent in our society today — it will take a renewing of our minds, individually and collectively, as the New Age implies. To reverse the trend, the alternative is like an upsidedown spiral of lies — there comes a time when the whole collapses from its own weight.

The renewing of one's mind means re-positioning our concepts of Reality. How basically important this is, especially to those of us who are bringing into life our human kind who will be translating their concepts of truth according to their convictions as they have learned them from their forebears. True understanding of the laws of life will be their responsibility as it is ours today. We are all living in the now — yesterday is but a memory of the way we reacted to life yesterday — tomorrow is but a projection of our convictions today — true or false.

Each of us is unique in the Mind of God. We have a purpose and that purpose is not an exact copy of the purpose of any other soul — no more than a fingerprint has an exact copy in the millions of people who populate this globe. The one thing we have in common is that our lives are One with the Mind of our Creator. We have to learn this position. It has to become a conviction. God did not make a mistake in His plan. How unrealistic it is to feel that somehow we were born to fail in our purpose in life. God must have an unbiased law governing His creative plan. If man is to be an extension of His Self, his plan of creation does not permit an imperfect soul of the human race which, under law, has to become an image of our Creator. This could not be possible if we were not to have freedom of choice.

An image of God is not one that must lean on any other Source than that provided by the Divine Laws of God. I believe we all must come to this understanding. This is what I mean by re-positioning our concepts of Reality. We were created to be successful. How can we fulfill that promise other than by using the creative word with which we are endowed, constructively. Surely not by looking at ourselves as misfits — diseased — unfortunate — yes, even though appearances seem to prove this so. If that is the kind of life we are so-called 'stuck with', individually and collectively, how did it happen if not by the Law of Cause and Effect? The creative thought-word-idea is and forever will be the only way to correct any negative situation not to our liking. This is the formula we have been using ignorantly to get us into the situation in which we find ourselves — and by using this same formula correctly we can get ourselves out of it and into the one we were originally designed to enjoy.

As the Scripture notes, symbolically, we are all 'prodigal sons' who have been taken in, so to speak, by appearances that speak so loudly of another power that seems to compete with the Principle of Divine Mind. This erroneous attitude of our beliefs is symbolized by the story of Adam, the first man, when instead of eating of the tree in the midst of the garden he began to eat of the tree of 'good and evil', thereby setting up the false belief of something called the devil or opposing power. 'The devil' is a liar and the father of it' — if we can accept the Master's teaching. The tree in the midst of the garden is the 'Tree of Life' that indwells us all as our conscience, and our conscience is none other than the Christ Principle or 'Lord God' as I have indicated more than once above.

Since our thoughts are always creating something — our collective thoughts are unequivocally responsible for the character of our civilization today. It must be clear that by the same inborn power and freedom of choice, and an open mind to truth or Reality, mankind can turn the tide of destructive tendencies that are plainly being outpictured in every quarter of the globe at this moment. Wise old King Solomon discovered that 'understanding' was indeed the most important possession one could have if he would have peace and happiness and the same in the hereafter.

Our souls are cast in eternity — our bodies are here today as an instrument — a function for the soul's use in this classroom of its progressive journey toward perfection — which an image must become before it can complete the cycle of its being (Alpha and Omega).

Needless to ask, does the reader ever wonder what the transition of the soul called death means in terms of an after-life? The answer — the writer can only pass on what has come to him in times of dedicated meditation. The souls of us are our real selves. They represent our memory and an idea in the Mind of God. The degree of its ability to function on this plane of life depends largely upon the brain mechanism passed on to it through heredity, as that, too, is under the law of Progression. The Bible speaks of it as the 'sins of our forefathers (or ignorance of truth) are passed on to us unto the third and fourth generations'. This is according to the genes of matter. However, the things that belong to the factual world of effects cannot and do not go with the soul in its transition. Only that which belongs to the memory in the soul's consciousness of truth finds itself in the hereafter where it exists among those of like position in consciousness.

I am saying that souls find their own mental level in the after-life as they do on the plane of matter. The phrase, 'you can't take it with you' means only our mental position survives so-called death. When our souls feel the urge for further experience on this plane of matter there will be another transition, and though we do not realize what is taking place, we awaken to a new life under the law of attraction. The soul then begins its new life classroom in a comparable condition for its progressive development. Never can one escape the law of progression on this or the other side of the vale. The souls of loved ones who are opposed in their convictions will naturally drift to those like themselves — 'to each his own' there, as here. They will be back into a physical and mental classroom 'to learn more of Reality'.

As I have indicated, Universal Laws of Life fill all space, as does the Mind of God. As for myself, I expect to find in my after-life only those mental convictions that I held in earth's conditions that coincide with the Universal Laws of Life. I, too, as everyone, have 'unfinished business', so to speak, that must be fulfilled, for we are still on an eternal pathway of learning how to live life constructively. As I have said before, the souls of us are 'cast in eternity' not to fail in our purpose in life.

We must come to discern Life — Truth — or Reality for what it is — not as it often appears to be. We must distinguish the relationship of First Cause and secondary cause which we so often blame for our undesirable conditions. We must recognize 'both sides of the coin'. It is this realism that makes King Solomon's advice so important to mankind, for 'understanding' makes all the difference in a person's position in life.

The sometimes hard lessons described in the biographical sketch of my life called, "The Straightening Path", currently up for publication, is seldom matched by boys of my age when I was drinking up adventure and experience (over half way around the world at thirteen) the 'hard way'. Yes, they were lessons I had to learn. I have come to consider these lessons as blessings in disguise. Is it coincidental that I became motherless at five, with a good father (a carpenter and part-time minister of the gospel) back in the eighteen hundreds? And now, in my eighty-eighth years, I feel so strongly impelled to write this message — hopefully to the many who are ready for the renewing of their minds concerning the Reality of Life which the New Age implies.

I feel accidents are non-existent, consequently, the writing of this book is in the framework of 'unfinished business'. Every time I go back over what I have written I get an uplift and seldom do I have to make changes in the truths I have transcribed — only in the improvement of my language. Does this add up to anything constructive in the reader's mind?

What are some of the truths that reflect my outlook? Are my prayers (affirmations) answered? How do I approach my philosophy of life? Perhaps the daily mealtime blessing which I formulated is representative of my convictions:

"WE THANK THEE, FATHER, FOR THIS FOOD AND FOR THE MANY BLESSINGS THOU HAST BESTOWED UPON US — FOR THE PERFECT HEALTH, YOUTH, ABUNDANCE AND RIGHT ADJUSTMENT WHICH IS OURS TO SHARE — FOR THE PERFECT EXPRESSION OF THE FIVE PHYSICAL SENSES — THE PSYCHIC NATURE — THE SPIRITUAL UNDERSTANDING — AND THE PERFECT INFLOW OF THY HEALING LIFE FORCES INTO EVERY CELL AND FUNCTION OF OUR BODIES. WE THANK THEE, FATHER, THESE QUALITIES WE ARE, CAN DO AND BE THROUGH THY CREATIVE CHRIST PRINCIPLE WHICH ABIDES IN US ALL. AND SO IT IS.

As the above implies, this is 'Practicing the Presence' and the fruits prove its efficacy. To those of us who are rearing families, I believe the following will not only be of interest but will point clearly to what must be done with our lives, as well as indicate how the creative principle of life works in practice.

"Opportunity isn't something that knocks on our door, then if we do not answer goes away forever. No. Opportunity is always before us. Why, then, is it that so many people constantly fail? I believe it is because of the position they take — one should reposition himself in consciousness. Many times opportunity is right before our eyes and we look right through it. Opportunity doesn't know age — it doesn't know whether we are male or female. It doesn't rest on education or environment. It isn't a matter of where we were born. Opportunity is always available, but we must be alert to recognize it."

Perhaps if you do not see opportunity around you should take a new position. Try to reposition yourself as you would like to be — experiencing what you would like to experience. Try this experiment: Mentally draw a picture of yourself as you feel yourself to be. You may be surprised to find that you do not have a good mental picture of yourself. You may find it very difficult to draw yourself from a mental concept. What are you really saying about yourself? You are saying, "I have no image of myself."

If you have no image of yourself, of course, you cannot draw yourself in mind or on paper. Try to image yourself as you are and then reposition yourself in mind and see yourself as you would like to be. This takes practice but it can be very worthwhile.

Many people are completely unaware that they are constantly making excuses and alibis for themselves. Many people have excuses for not demonstrating and alibis for not manifesting. But excuses and alibis are not sound reasons. We should sit down and say to ourselves: "Today I want no alibi for failures to manifest what I want. I am going to be honest with myself. I want to know the reason I am not demonstrating. I want to reposition myself in consciousness. I want to impress my Creative Christ Consciousness with the actions of well-being and happiness".*

It was metaphysics (a combination of mental and physical understanding) that confirmed my feeling that all was not true that greeted the eye. Metaphysics lead me to a clearer conception of Reality and the laws that govern 'It'. When one becomes fully cognizant with its meaning and the benefits one acquires, he is said to be imbued with its science. And whether he or she realizes it or not, this individual has become an advocate of Religious Science or Science of Mind.

There is no promise that one may, through an understanding of its workings, dispel pain and suffering. But practice of the truths (practice of the Presence) turns negative thoughts that we have been impressing upon the subconscious into constructive ones that outpicture after their kind. In other words, right use of the Spiritual Laws that govern the Universe instills 'faith', then faith becomes established in the whole position of our convictions.

The law of attraction automatically attracts friends, satisfactory situations, and escapes from what could become disasters. Friends often call it luck but deep down in one's soul comes another name for it. My own life records experiences that have proven my point time and time again. I have no alibis, no excuses. Call them growing pains or what you will, but I thank the "Father" every day of my life for now I realize they are really blessings in disguise.

There are those, even in the several branches of my own

* Dr. Frank E. Richelieu

family, who consider these things unrealistic. In my family there has always been the practice of freedom of choice regarding our religious affiliations. Of course my choice has been a metaphysical one of long standing.

If you have been wondering what results have been outpicturing in my life as a consequence of my convictions, I will say, without going back to experiences I have had in years long past, but to some very, very recent ones.

1. Twenty-three days in the hospital for a double surgery operation, with seven days in 'Intensive Care'. During this time it took quite a bit of medical 'know-how' to keep me around (or so they thought).

2. During my long stay in the hospital my wife was concerned about the tremendous bill we were certain to receive upon my release. After I came home she went back to the hospital to find out what the charges were going to be and they told her they had already been taken care of. Of course outward appearances would seem to indicate other reasons but they add up to inner causes, I am sure.

3. Due to a water slick I ran into while driving, I lost control of my car and ploughed into a plate glass store window at about thirty miles per hour — necessitating twelve stitches on the top of my head from flying glass. There were no other personal injuries. Of course I lost my '68 Olds but I was getting ready to turn it in on another car anyway. On my way across the curb and into the window, I glanced off the front of a car parked at the curb. There appeared to be no one in the car but I understand a woman was seated on the front seat on the curb side. Before I left the scene I was told she was not hurt, just shaken up a bit. However, the same people filed a suit for $125,000 punitive damages. They could not prove irresponsibility or negligence on my part and my insurance company took care of the damage to their car and the

whole matter was settled well within my insurance coverage.

4. Not long ago I stumbled and fell flat on my face on a cement walk which was edged with brick. There was no way to break my weight during the fall. I had on glasses and they were not even cracked — they were merely thrown off during my descent.

5. Recently I stumbled again, this time over a milk carrying case on our front porch — which is about a foot off the ground. Again no breaking of my weight during the fall and no injuries other than a small scratch on the forehead. My glasses were thrown to the side a second time. Many say, including my wife, that I am unbelievably lucky.

It seems my whole life has been one of close calls — as far back as I can remember. Why? I believe I know the answer. It took me a long time to learn the fruitful response of a proffered hand of friendship, too. And may I say the change from a reticent attitude of inferiority to one of outgiving understanding and 'right adjustment' began with my acceptance of the metaphysical approach to Spiritual Reality.

Is it profitable? Emphatically, yes! And more, it holds the answer to a deteriorating society and its ecology.

Recently, I listened to a noted and widely-travelled lecturer — an authority on world affairs in its various departments of social well-being. He drew a resounding applause and that, too, from a comparatively religious audience. The essence of his subject was that he 'pulls no punches' — 'he tells it as it is'.

Please note the difference in my reaction to most of his audience and, also, please remember that I said previously that I was the 'writer' of this message and not the 'author'.

I am deeply commited to the truth that 'telling it as it is' is not possible when we are limited by the evidence of our senses — when Reality means the factual world of effects.

I have, throughout this book, been endeavoring to tell it as it really is in Divine Mind for the only Reality possible is a Spiritual Reality. How many times have you been disappointed in placing your confidence in human beings or their trappings? How often do we find the so-called 'well-bred' sitting in the seats where 'character' should be? Culture cannot take the place of character when character is linked with morality.

I have not found any valid reason to alter the truths that have come to me in times of deep meditation.

GLOSSARY OF TERMS AND THEIR MEANING

As Used in This Treatise

"In the Beginning" — The Beginning of Consciousness — the first activation of an idea in the Mind of God or the "I Am" awareness in the mind of *man.*

"The Real Church" — "The Temple of the Living God is the soul of man — Its minister is "the Creative Christ Principle" or *"The Word of God"* which occupies the dominating seat of the Spiritual Government of heaven and of earth — Our conscience which is always at the center and seat of *our* consciousness — never outside.

"The Church according to the letter" — A symbolic church organized according to a dim understanding of reality by ancient peoples, which persists to the present day, and which resists the real nature of the Principles it espouses, namely: *progress in spiritual matters.*

"The Conscious Mind" — Is the directing center of the Soul consciousness of man. It chooses — It wills in exact accordance with its convictions — It directs the subconscious part of its administration, both directly and indirectly, in respect to the involuntary operations of its material organism. Its seat of operations is the brain, thence the heart, thence the solar-plexis. The heart supplies the emotion — the solar-plexis

reflects an idea through the sympathetic systems of nerves to the various involutory functions of the organism. Its monitor and guide is the moral principle within or the creative Christ principle which does not dictate but validates the *"word"* as *human* consciousness chooses to interpret it.

"CREATION" — The inception of any idea in mind — or imagination — or consciousness — "the Word made flesh." The process begins in imagination — discerned by the mind but not seen by physical eyes *until* it is evolved to the point of manifestation.

"Death" — Denotes the dissolution of effect — Dissolution is its nature. *What it dissolves can be heavenly or hellish.* It has no power in itself. Its seeming power is a derivative of the power behind freedom of choice or the will of human consciousness.

"Divine Plan" — To extend and *multiply Itself* through the instrumentality of Itself, i.e., the dynamic phase of Itself by the expediency of *being*, in imagination, that which it wills to create. Operates through the polarity of the Trinity of Cause — or Will to be — and the effect.

"Discernment" — Mental seeing — psychological cognition — extra-sensory perception — intuitive imagery — All interpretive faculties of the soul.

"Effect" — That which results from the *initial* Creative Word or Will. It may be of spiritual nature, psychological, or metaphysical or material effect; depending upon the purpose *embodied in the initial creative* Word. When effect is disconnected from its Cause it is said to die.

"Extra-Sensory Perception" — A variously developed intuitive faculty or sixth sense with which all, in degree, are endowed. It can be developed in the same

manner that any art is developed. It works best in an atmosphere of silence and in concentrated and relaxed meditation. It reaches its height of perfection in the realm of *spiritual* understanding. It has nothing to do with deception or charlatanism or fortune telling — which, is an erroneous application of the principle sometimes by the unscrupulous.

"Heaven" — A state of consciousness — an effect of righteous thinking and acting — a belief in *One* overall *Principle* and end purpose *of good* and allegiance to That Principle.

"Hell" — A state of consciousness — an effect of error in thinking and acting — a belief in two opposing Principles, namely: Good and Evil. A lack of understanding of Divine Law.

"The Hereafter", Our Identity therein — A state of consciousness in which the soul finds itself possessed of its real body which is patterned after the ideal, in degree it thought and lived that Ideal while on the material plane in a material body. A simile exists in material nature — with one exception — the lowly caterpillar is transformed into a beautiful butterfly *without* its own knowledge of how it is done; (man *learns how* it is accomplished). Our ideals of an eternal nature are the treasures we lay up in the heavens of our consciousness. Abstract Reality is the soul and heart of nature. It is the only quality that survives the transition called death.

"Holy Bible — An inspirationally written textbook concerning the way Divine Law works. It is historical — it is symbolical — it deals with the Divine Standard of rules applicable to all mankind. It has an inner and outer meaning. The inner or Spiritual meaning holds infinitely deeper significance than the outer letter — in relation to the maturing faculties of the *hu-*

man intellect. It has a constructive message for all who seek the Truth. The channels for its wisdom have been many but the minds of those channels are One.

"Humanity" — Is the highest evolved idea of the multitudinous forms which the *"Creative Word* assumes, in its progressive unfoldment of the souls of mankind. Mankind in themselves are endowed with reason and freedom of choice — and are reflections in essence in accordance with their lights.

"I" — Is Principle — Static, in relation to its creation — Name of God — Name of the first person — in whose name the human "I" speaks.

"I Am" — The dynamic phase of God — The Divine Principle of creation — The activating phase of Principle — Principle becomes its creation out of the substance of Itself — It is the *Divine Name*, when in the creative process. It is The Lord God — The Christ — The verb "to be".

"Inspiration" — A verb denoting the activation of an inner Source of awareness — a feeling of a knowingness accompanying an idea or light without the necessity of reason which is applied later with success in relation to the limited understanding of the human intellect. Only one of the avenues through which the intuitive faculties of man have access to the overshadowing Intelligence of God.

"Life" — Has no beginning nor ending — It is not limited by time nor space — It is Substance Eternal — It is spirit — It was never born nor ever can die. It is the essence of all experience. It has a nature of *non-being* (static) and a nature of *being* (dynamic). It is synonymous with God.

"Metaphysics" — The Semantics of Reality. That classified pursuit of knowledge which is not limited by physical means of measurement, only by the degree

of development of the mental and imaginative faculties or the psychological and spiritual faculties or the sixth sense. All of which functions on the abstract side of nature which, has its own peculiar standards of measurement. The knowledge it sheds is the saving Principle of mankind.

"Physical Science" — That classified pursuit of knowledge that is limited by the extent of its ability to measure the physical aspects or effects of abstract Cause.

"Resurrection" — Is a term used to indicate the raising of soul consciousness or understanding to more closely experience and appreciate the reality of its relationship to its Maker in whose image it is created. It is Metaphysics, being understood.

"Salvation" — The saving of anything (the soul included) from any condition or experience not in keeping with its purpose of existence — a purpose in the Mind of Divine Intelligence.

"Satan" — An offspring of the belief in two opposing powers — non-Principle — "A lie and the father of it" — non-existent, without power except as it is given power by the conscious mind.

"Soul" — The essence of any idea — the essence or idea or light of man — created perfect, in the image of Divine Intelligence — an extention of the Divine plan of creation — of an eternal nature in the creative process of becoming. "Created one step below the angels", in order that it may function on the material plane of nature and learn by experience.

"The Subconscious Mind" — The activating principle of the creative thought-word — its operations are carried out on the unseen or abstract side of the creative process. It is the servant of the conscious mind — it acts upon orders — It does not question. Its definiteness, efficiency or expediency will reflect the power,

sincerity and clear-cut desire behind the creative Word. It is linked with the Word as effects is linked with Cause. It has no prejudices. It carries out the will to live and be productive of something, good, bad or indifferent — It is unlimited through lack of means or instrumentalities. It has no religious scruples; Saint or sinner all, are under its Law.

"*Tithing*" — Returning a portion of the fruit of any activity back to the source which gave birth to it, which, in every case is the idea behind the activity. It forms a receptive expectancy in the human mind.

"*Truth*" — Is Reality — First Cause — Substance — Universal Spirit — Universal Law — Divine Principle — Divine Intelligence, Power, Life. Is Omnipresent, Omniscient and Omnipowerful God. Is All in All — Father of Lights — Source of ideas — whose name is "I" and who is static until It moves to create — then It is dynamic and Its name becomes "I Am" or "Being". It is the activating Principle called "The Christ of God" — "Who is given all-power in heaven and earth" — "Through which all things are made that are made" and "without which no thing is made that is made". The Lord God — "The Way Shower". It is all these and more.

"*The Word*" — The "Word" or "Thought-word of God" is the creative instrumentality — the activating Principle — The Father's will to become manifest — the dynamic phase of Divine Principle or God. It is the Christ of God — the First Born — the Only Son, and is "the Light that lighteth every man that cometh into the world". It is the First Cause or movement in creation by the "Father of Lights". It initials the cause that becomes an effect. Its product is pure at point of inception. Its nature is progressive Spirit — Pure Light — Pure Idea. It is the life in man that identifies itself as "I". It looks out of your eyes and mine. It not only initials, but maintains that which it initials by *becoming* and *being* that which it initials. It initials and names an idea as it is launched into the creative processes of nature by the number or rate of vibratory impulses of which an idea or light is composed. It names our children. It named you!

TWO ANCIENT SYMBOLS OF THE CREATIVE PROCESS

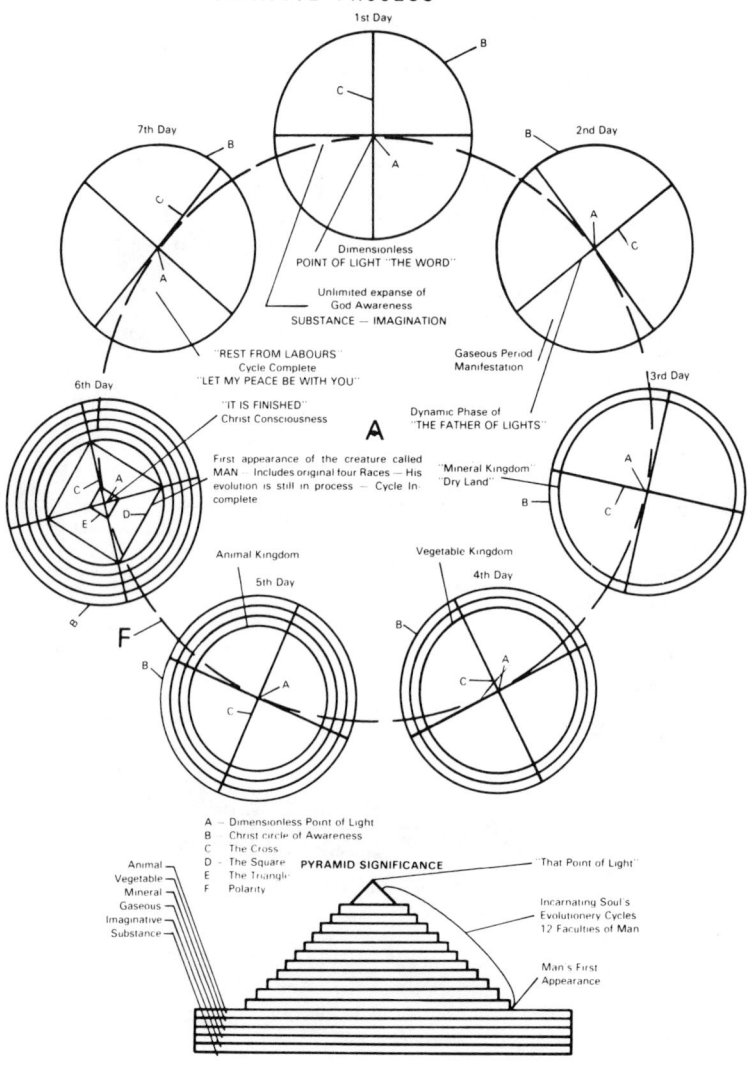

1st Day
Dimensionless
POINT OF LIGHT "THE WORD"
Unlimited expanse of
God Awareness
SUBSTANCE — IMAGINATION

2nd Day
Gaseous Period
Manifestation
Dynamic Phase of
"THE FATHER OF LIGHTS"

3rd Day
"Mineral Kingdom"
"Dry Land"

4th Day
Vegetable Kingdom

5th Day
Animal Kingdom

6th Day
First appearance of the creature called MAN — Includes original four Races — His evolution is still in process — Cycle Incomplete

7th Day
"REST FROM LABOURS"
Cycle Complete
"LET MY PEACE BE WITH YOU"
"IT IS FINISHED"
Christ Consciousness

A — Dimensionless Point of Light
B — Christ circle of Awareness
C — The Cross
D — The Square
E — The Triangle
F — Polarity

Animal
Vegetable
Mineral
Gaseous
Imaginative
Substance

PYRAMID SIGNIFICANCE

"That Point of Light"
Incarnating Soul's
Evolutionary Cycles
12 Faculties of Man
Man's First
Appearance

183

Earth's Solar Orb (the still, cold and perfectly balanced in-dwelling "spiritual White Light of Divine Intelligence") A

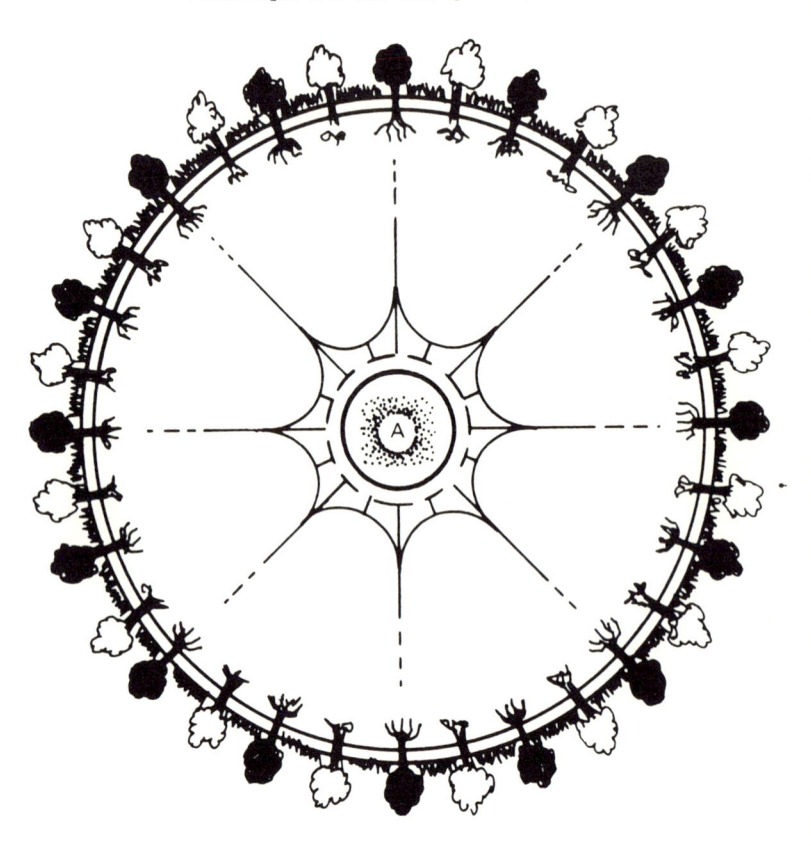

When one mentally "back-tracks" a single ray of the billions of vibratory impulses that earth's Solar Orb sends forth, we not only find they support all living things on earth but identifies them mathematically by the number and rate of impulses.

FREEDOM OF CHOICE
GOD'S GIFT TO MAN

No organization — moral or otherwise — that circumvents a person's freedom to choose — whether it be accomplished mentally or physically — is violating an ordinance of God.

Millions around this world have lost mental freedom in the subtle way of dogma and not so subtle way of requiring one to consign one's innocent children to a faith that may not have been their choice in later years.

I am utterly aghast at what is going on in Ireland today — a tragic example of thousands that, but for their teachability would have never chosen to quarrel with members of another's 'moral guiding institution' who profess the same God. It just takes eight words to qualify my statement! "God does not compete with Himself." — according to my way of looking at it.

India's slavery and the wrong interpretation of God's Spiritual intent for makind has resulted in starvation — disease — and death.

Renouncing the World is not compatible with Jesus' teaching or the Divine Laws of the 'Christ of God' which He embodied.

CYCLE OF BEING

A circle of light some call Mind.
A dimensionless point, a spark Divine.
A gaseous mist with chemistry sublime,
Brings an atom into space and time.
A crystal forms, pestle and bowl
To serve as base, life's class of the soul.
Rain descends, a molecule dawns,
An amoeba wriggles, a saurian yawns.
A dinosaur lumbers, and man appears:
Flesh, as the animal, but higher geared.
In the image of God, God said he's made.
His body the sum of the elements He laid.
Lord of the earth and all of the same
Though he must find for himself how he is made,
For, 'tis he alone that maketh his bed.
Comes aware of himself then, reason is fed:
Fire from flint and an urge to create
Examines himself and the animals he ate:
Thence to the skies his thoughts explore,
Whence he came and must come to adore.
On the wings of time his class lets out,
Back to his Source he must be about.
Back to the dust his body must go but,
The light of the soul, this is not so!
The essence of life is the light thereof
And the Father of Lights is the Father above.

F. Stewart Merritt

FINIS

Permanent spiritual qualities are not built in a day and spiritual qualities underlie all manifestation. But the light or idea that converts one from traveling in the wrong *direction* to one in harmony with God's purpose comes in the "twinkling of an eye". It is well to remember the windows and the doors of the minds of the souls of men must be wide open.

"The Master appears only when the disciple is ready." The Master is the Spirit of Truth that speaks from within. He says: "Come let us reason together."

Jesus was thirty-three when He left the scene and He said: "If I go I shall come again." Have you discovered what He meant?

Not in physical form, of course, but a mental concept from the Christ seat of our conscience — the skies of mind. Yes, the Christ Principle is at one with the metaphysical teaching — a science that puts one's life cycle in harmony with the Reality of life.

And, finally the writer hopefully has interpreted this message as it has come to him without reservations or compromising of the Truth as it is given to him to understand it.